THE BATTLE
— FOR —
REDEMPTION

A WALK THROUGH THE BIBLE

CHRIS WEBBER

Copyright © 2018 Christopher Webber

All rights reserved. No part of this publication may be reproduced, distributed, or transmitted in any form or by any means, including photocopying, recording, or other electronic or mechanical methods, without the prior written permission of the publisher, except in the case of brief quotations embodied in reviews and certain other non-commercial uses permitted by copyright law. For information regarding permission, write to Chris Webber, Nichols Street Church of Christ, c. 979.240.4685 or cwebber@harding.edu.

Cover art by Germancreative at http://depositphotos.com

Unless otherwise indicated, all Scripture quotations are from The Holy Bible, New International Version ® NIV ®

Copyright © 1973, 1978, 1984, 2011 by Biblica, Inc.™ Used by permission. All rights reserved worldwide. www.zondervan.com

The "NIV" and "New International Version" are trademarks registered in the United States Patent and Trademark Offices by Biblica, Inc.™

Scripture quotations marked (ESV) are from The Holy Bible, English Standard Version ®, copyright © 2001 by Crossway Bibles, a publishing ministry of Good News Publishers. Used by permission. All rights reserved.

Scripture quotations marked (MSG) are from THE MESSAGE. Copyright © 1993, 1994, 1995, 1996, 2000, 2001, 2002. Used by permission of NavPress Publishing Group.

Free Vectors Designed by: https://www.vecteezy.com and by Freepik from www.flaticon.com

ISBN-13: 978-0-578-42162-9

ISBN-10: 0-578-42162-3

CONTENTS

Acknowledgements — v
Forward — vii
Introduction — ix

Part One: Start — 1

  CHAPTER ONE: Creation — 3

  CHAPTER TWO: The Fall — 7

Part Two: Family Figures — 26

  CHAPTER THREE: Abraham & Sarah — 27

  CHAPTER FOUR: Isaac & Rebekah — 36

  CHAPTER FIVE: Jacob & Rachel — 45

  CHAPTER SIX: Joseph — 62

  CHAPTER SEVEN: Moses — 89

  CHAPTER EIGHT: Shaping a Nation Gods at War — 105

Part Three: Back to the Promised Land — 128

  CHAPTER NINE: Joshua — 129

  CHAPTER TEN: Judges — 141

Part Four: Do Good 160

    CHAPTER ELEVEN: Kings 161

    CHAPTER TWELVE: Prophets 177

Part Five: The New Testament 204

    CHAPTER THIRTEEN: Jesus 205

    CHAPTER FOURTEEN: Church 230

    CHAPTER FIFTEEN: The Letters 240

    CHAPTER SIXTEEN: Revelation 261

AFTERWORD: What Next? 270

About the Author 273

ACKNOWLEDGEMENTS

I am grateful for the team of people who have helped make this dream become a reality. Without them this book would not be possible. It truly requires a village to help make greatness transpire.

Thanks to . . .

My wife, Katie Sue Webber, for being incredibly patient during this journey of writing. I could not have asked for a better wife. I am incredibly blessed to be your husband.

My parents, Kelly and Jackie Webber, for their constant support and providing a wonderful life for me. They not only believed in my dreams but helped make them financially possible.

My son, Carson John Webber, for being an inspiration for this book. I pray that you fall in love with God's Word and that you choose to have a relationship with Him.

Russ Womack, Faralee Pozo and Carey Scott for being an unimaginable editing team. You took the bones that I gave you and put flesh on them. I am forever grateful for each of you.

Nichols Street Church of Christ for believing in me and pursuing God alongside me.

FORWARD

By Russ Womack

Author Chris Webber masterfully clears the difficulty in comprehending the Bible in his book *The Battle for Redemption, A Walk Through the Bible*. Written in a straightforward, chronological, and easy to understand format, it seamlessly removes any confusion or barriers to the most important book in the world.

I can say with absolute assurance that this is a must read for all audiences. Whether you've read the bible one thousand times or have yet to open to the book of Genesis, *The Battle for Redemption, A Walk Through the Bible* presents a clear and concise layout that breathes encouragement, inspiration, humor, and wonder. You can't help but feel drawn to reading the Bible after contemplating upon the words in this book.

With each turn of the page, Chris sets you on the dusty streets of Galilee as you walk alongside people who are just like you. They are relatable and transparent, fallible and human, and just as real today as they were when they walked beside Jesus. The scriptures come alive and the messages are coherent, and any thought of putting the Bible back away on the shelf is evaporated as curiosity and discernment rise up in your heart. You'll find yourself immersed in the stories, enlightened by facts that you never quite understood, and you'll find yourself falling in love with God.

INTRODUCTION

The Bible is daunting, confusing, and it's so massive that there's not enough time to actually sit down and read it.

These are statements that I've heard over and over working in ministry. Countless people have told me that they do not understand how the stories in the Bible fit together. And many people outside of the church have told me that they don't understand how a book written so many years ago still has relevance today for people's lives.

In this book, I will show you that reading the Bible doesn't have to be daunting or confusing. I'll even show you that the Bible is extremely relevant today and just as much relevant now as it was when it was written to its original audience thousands of years ago.

I have had the privilege to study the Bible at Harding University and attain a bachelor's degree in Youth and Family Ministry before moving on to graduate school at Dallas Theological Seminary where I earned a master's degree in Christian Education. I've dedicated my life to teach the Bible to people. Luckily, I married a woman who is just as passionate and in love with God as I am (and she's pretty too!).

Over the course of this book I will break down the Bible for you and show you how the books fit together chronologically. I'll also explain to you some of the hidden truths that many people just skip right over while reading the Bible (things like the women who paid for Jesus' bills). Trust me, stay on this ride and you will come out enthralled with God's Word.

While writing this book, I have been blessed with an incredible team of people who have given feedback on the manuscript. The best thing about this book is whether you've read ten pages or one hundred pages you'll be fascinated by the depth, wonder, and whimsy of the incredible book we call the Bible.

Here's the deal.

If you stick with this, I promise you that the Bible will look very different to you. Not that I will be adding to or taking away from this God-breathed book, but that we will walk through the Bible in such a way that you'll be able to grasp the flow of all the books. That's my goal. I wrote this with you in mind.

I want you to fly with me way up high in the air so that you can see the Bible from a different angle. Have you ever flown before or maybe ridden high on an amusement ride? Can you remember that feeling when everything below you got just that much smaller—the buildings, cars, people? My promise to you is that you're going to gain a different perspective on the scriptures. You'll see the entire Bible in panoramic view. The biblical stories will come to life. This book is going to become one of your greatest treasures, pointing you toward the Bible and helping you gain a broader perspective for it.

INTRODUCTION

Don't be the person who misses out on this experience. I've already told you what you'll be getting yourself into. Take a leap of faith and join me on this journey.

So, there you have it. You have followed me this long and that shows that you're dedicated and that this is for you. The Bible was written to reveal God to people like you, me, and well . . . everyone. My purpose in writing this book is to simply highlight who God is and share Him with you.

Find a comfy place in your house, barn, spacecraft, pool . . . Whatever place is most comfortable for you and go there. Take a break from your busy schedule and relax as we embark on a journey into the Beginning

PART ONE
Start

CREATION

CHAPTER ONE

In the beginning God created the heavens and the earth. Now the earth was formless and empty, darkness was over the surface of the deep, and the Spirit of God was hovering over the waters. And God said, "Let there be light," and there was light. Genesis 1:1-3 NIV

The universe was a blank canvas.
Then God began to paint the world into picture.
He made every single thing good.

With God's mighty hand He stretched out the land and the sea and placed animals and creatures in His order. There was distinction between night and day; land and sea; good and evil. God's blueprint for creation had come to fruition.

Next, God made something that was different from the rest of His creation.

Humanity.

In what appeared to be perfection, God found it lacking of something. In the final stage of His plan, He reached down to the earth and dug up dirt. Molding it into a human figure, God held it to His lips and breathed life into its nostrils.

> *Then God said, "Let us make mankind in our image, in our likeness, so that they may rule over the fish in the sea and the birds in the sky, over the livestock and all the wild animals, and over all the creatures that move along the ground."*
>
> *So God created mankind in his own image,*
> *In the image of God he created him;*
> *Male and female he created them.*
>
> *God blessed them and said to them, "Be fruitful and increase in number; fill the earth and subdue it. Rule over the fish in the sea and the birds in the sky and over every living creature that moves on the ground." Genesis 1:26-28 NIV*

Do you notice the repetition?
God said that He was going to do something . . .

Let's make man in our image;
And they will make babies and rule the land.
And then He does it.
So God created man in His image,
To make babies and rule the land.

The repetition is important, and occurs throughout the Bible; God consistently proves to follow through with His Word, even from the very beginning.

But, let's jump back to the "Our image" part of the scripture we just read.

CREATION

God is the Creator and He wasn't alone?
Exactly.
Sort of.

God is a Triune God, meaning, three persons: God (the Father), God (the Son) and God (the Spirit). "Tri" meaning three and "une" meaning unity. Each person of the Trinity is distinct, but together form one God.

Everything that God had created prior to humanity was good, but once He made humanity, things began to look very different. God gave His very own image to a new kind of creation. The Father, Spirit, and Son united to create two humans after their likeness; male and female He created them.

This is a game changer in the design process of the world. Nothing to that point had claimed an attribute of God.

Then, in a bold move, the Trinity (Father, Son, and Spirit) gave dominion over the earth to the world's first couple, Adam and Eve, and placed them in the Garden of Eden.

The world was theirs.
It was figuratively in their hands.
What a powerful position to be in.

The God of the cosmos, and the Creator of all things, handed over His grand creation to this newly-created couple with two goals in mind: have children and take care of the place that He had gifted them.

Imagine that you have a child.
This child needs a place to live.

Out of the kindness of your heart you gift your child a house.

Now, you would urge this child to take care of it.
You would explain that this house is a gift.
You would expect for your child to take care of it.

Your child would need to clean up after itself, mop the floors, mow the yard, and trim the hedges, etc., because the house is a gift and you would expect your child to treat it with more respect than something attained by its own means.

Now, back to that garden.
It was a gift.

God gave this new creation over to His children. He didn't want Adam and Eve to just sit and look pretty. They were given a job. The job description, you ask? Protect the land, cultivate it, rule over it, and make babies. God gave this gift with the intention that Adam and Eve would take care of it.

Now, on to that evil seedless tree.

THE FALL

CHAPTER TWO

Did God really say, "You must not eat from any tree in the garden"? Genesis 3:1 NIV

———————————

Three chapters.
That's all it took.

Three chapters in the first book of the Bible and we find humankind sinning for the very first time. Where did this evil even come from? We just read about God's creation and that everything was good!

> *God saw all that he had made, and it was very good. And there was evening, and there was morning—the sixth day. Genesis 1:31 NIV*

Six days into creation and everything was still good. The seventh day was stamped with God's blessing, so apparently things were still going well. So again, where did evil come from?

Prior to Genesis 3, peace covered the cosmos. But then, God's Heavenly government had a breach. Lucifer, one of the head angels, became prideful and corrupt and was cast out of Heaven. It was in an instant that his name changed from Lucifer *"morning star"* to Satan *"adversary"* and he began to see that his power was limited. But, just as he violated God's authority in Heaven, he did the same on earth by tempting humanity to sin and follow in his rebellion.

> *Satan:* "Did God really say, 'You must not eat from any tree in the garden'?"
>
> *Eve:* "We may eat fruit from the trees in the garden, but God did say, 'You must not eat fruit from the tree that is in the middle of the garden, and you must not touch it, or you will die.'"
>
> *Satan:* "You will not certainly die, for God knows that when you eat from it your eyes will be opened, and you will be like God, knowing good and evil."
>
> *When the woman saw that the fruit of the tree was good for food and pleasing to the eye, and also desirable for gaining wisdom, she took some and ate it. She also gave some to her husband, who was with her, and he ate it. Then the eyes of both of them were opened, and they realized they were naked; so they sewed fig leaves together and made coverings for themselves. Genesis 3:1-7 NIV*

So, there it is.
God's newly-created world was infected.
And sin was the disease.

What was so bad about that tree?
Everything God created was good, right?

THE FALL

Jump back to Genesis 1.

> *The land produced vegetation: plants bearing seed according to their kinds and trees bearing fruit with seed in it according to their kinds. And God saw that it was good. Then God said, "I give you every seed-bearing plant on the face of the whole earth and every tree that has fruit with seed in it. They will be yours for food." Genesis 1:12, 29 NIV*

Plants with seed: Good. Check!
Plants without seeds: Bad. Check!

So, that clears things up a little bit.

Apparently, the forbidden tree was seedless. Which would mean, this tree could not be replicated. It couldn't bear offspring. God wouldn't want it to.

At this point in scripture, everything that was good could reproduce. Man's job was to cultivate the garden so that the vegetation could reproduce and be a food source and, more importantly, make babies with his wife to fill the earth.

But this forbidden tree.
That was not its purpose.
It couldn't be reproduced.
Its job was singular.

God wanted Adam and Eve to have the choice to follow Him or follow themselves. God wasn't going to force anyone to love Him. His love is sincere and pure. The purpose of this tree was to allow free will of humankind. Will you follow God or will you follow yourself?

> Then the man and his wife heard the sound of the Lord God as he was walking in the garden in the cool of the day, and they hid from the Lord God among the trees of the garden.
>
> God: "Where are you?"

(Side Note: God couldn't find Adam? The Creator of all things got lost in His own creation? God knew where Adam was, but He wanted to know where Adam's heart was. God is omnipresent, meaning "ever present". While we're at it, God is also omnipotent, "holds all authority", and omniscient, "all knowing.")

> Adam: "I heard you in the garden, and I was afraid because I was naked; so I hid."
>
> God: "Who told you that you were naked? Have you eaten from the tree that I commanded you not to eat from?"
>
> Adam: "The woman you put here with me—she gave me some fruit from the tree, and I ate it."
>
> God: "What is this you have done?"
>
> Eve: "The serpent deceived me, and I ate."
> Genesis 3:8-13 NIV

CONSEQUENCES

> So the Lord God said to the serpent, "Because you have done this, Cursed are you above all livestock and all wild animals! You will crawl on your belly and you will eat dust all the days of your life. And I will put enmity between you and the woman, and between your offspring and hers; he will crush your head, and you will strike his heel."

To the woman he said, "I will make your pains in childbearing very severe; with painful labor you will give birth to children. Your desire will be for your husband, and he will rule over you."

To Adam he said, "Because you listened to your wife and ate fruit from the tree about which I commanded you, 'You must not eat from it,' Cursed is the ground because of you; through painful toil you will eat food from it all the days of your life It will produce thorns and thistles for you, and you will eat the plants of the field. By the sweat of your brow you will eat your food until you return to the ground, since from it you were taken; for dust you are and to dust you will return." Genesis 3:14-19 NIV

LIKE ONE OF US

And the Lord God said, "The man has now become like one of us, knowing good and evil. He must not be allowed to reach out his hand and take also from the tree of life and eat, and live forever." So the Lord God banished him from the Garden of Eden to work the ground from which he had been taken. After he drove the man out, he placed on the east side of the Garden of Eden cherubim and a flaming sword flashing back and forth to guard the way to the tree of life. Genesis 3:22-24 NIV

CAIN AND ABEL

Soon after Adam and Eve were kicked out of the Garden of Eden, Eve became pregnant and gave birth to Cain and Abel and the sin problem had all but gone away.

> *Now Abel kept flocks, and Cain worked the soil. In the course of time Cain brought some of the fruits of the soil as an offering to the LORD. But, Abel brought fat portions from some of the firstborn of his flock. The LORD looked with favor on Abel and his offering, but on Cain and his offering he did not look with favor. So Cain was very angry, and his face was downcast. Genesis 4:2-5 NIV*

Abel's offering was accepted.
Cain's offering was not?
Cain worked the soil.
That was his job!
So, he gave of the ground he worked.
Abel works the flocks.
Naturally, he gave of the flocks he worked.
Where's the problem here?

> *Then the LORD said to Cain, "Why are you angry? Why is your face downcast? If you do what is right, will you not be accepted? But if you do not do what is right, sin is crouching at your door; it desires to have you, but you must master it."*
>
> *Now Cain said to his brother Abel, "Let's go out to the field." And while they were in the field, Cain attacked his brother Abel and killed him." Genesis 4:6-8 NIV*

Something deeper is going on here.
Abel gave out of abundance.
So did Cain.
But, Cain's gift was apparently less than par.

How do we know this?
Well, one, God didn't accept Cain's gift.
And, two, check out this verse in Hebrews 11.

THE FALL

> *By faith Abel offered to God a more acceptable sacrifice than Cain, through which he was commended as righteous, God commending him by accepting his gifts. Hebrews 11:4 NIV*

The issue wasn't that Cain gave a bad gift.
The author doesn't even settle on the gift.
It was the worshipful heart that made Abel's gift better.

Two seconds after Cain's gift was rejected he became angry with God and killed his brother. This shows his true attitude.

> *God:* "Where is your brother Abel?"
>
> *Cain:* "I don't know, am I my brother's keeper?"
>
> *God:* "What have you done? Listen! Your brother's blood cries out to me from the ground. Now, you are under a curse and driven from the ground, which opened its mouth to receive your brother's blood from your hand. When you work the ground, it will no longer yield its crops for you. You will be a restless wanderer on the earth."
>
> *Cain:* "My punishment is more than I can bear. Today you are driving me from the land, and I will be hidden from your presence; I will be a restless wanderer on the earth, and whoever finds me will kill me."
>
> *God:* "Not so; anyone who kills Cain will suffer vengeance seven times over." Then the Lord put a mark on Cain so that no one who found him would kill him. Genesis 4:9-15 NIV

That was a real conversation between Cain and God. How did he not realize God knew what he'd done?

God desires true worship.

Remember the gift from the last chapter?
You know, the house you gave to your "children"?
You gave that house to them out of an overflow of your love.

Now, imagine that you gave them this gift.
One of your children walks straight up to you.
They look you straight in the eyes.
They give you a half-hearted, "thanks" and walks away.

Would you be mad?
Or would you be frustrated?
Or quite possibly disgusted?

This house.
It's a pretty great house.
It's sturdy.
It's beautiful.
And, you put a lot of work into it.
Come on, you wanted it to be perfect for them.

God wanted a little more enthusiasm from Cain.
Cain's gift wasn't all that bad.
In reality, it was probably a pretty decent gift.
But, God knew the heart behind the gift.
And after his rejection we see his heart.

SETH

After Cain and Abel, Adam and Eve gave birth to Seth. Seth grew and married then had a son named Enosh. At that time men began to call on the name of the LORD (Genesis 4:26).

That's pretty much all we get.
No details about Cain and his influence.
No reasons why humans followed God again.
No background stories.

So, let's read on.

WAIT, WE MESSED UP AGAIN?

Now, in the story we get a ton of genealogy. The Bible traces humanity from Adam and Eve to a man named Noah and his family.

Remember that after God gave Adam and Eve the gift he held them to a promise? He told them to take care of the gift (the world) and to make babies (fill the earth). Well, that's exactly what they did. And after Seth married and had his own kids, his kids had kids and so on. The world began to be filled but not exactly to the standards that God had set.

Just like how Cain had a heart problem and became angry, so did many of his family's descendants and the world became a pretty corrupt place.

> *The LORD saw how great man's wickedness on the earth had become, and that every inclination of the thoughts of his heart was only evil all the time. The LORD was grieved that he had made man on the earth, and his heart was filled with pain. So the LORD said, "I will wipe mankind, whom I have created, from the face of the earth—men and animals, and creatures that move along the ground, and birds of the air—for I am grieved that I have made them." But Noah found favor in the eyes of the LORD. Genesis 6:5-8 NIV*

God's heart was filled with pain.
Did you catch that?

Think about it this way.
You gave an incredible gift to your kids.
They enjoyed it for a while.
But, they started getting bored of their gift.
They wanted to treat it however they wanted.
They didn't listen to how you told them to take care of it.
The carpet began to be filled with a sour stench.
Clothes were all over the floor.
The utilities all turned off due to lack of payment.
The weeds and bushes in the yard grew out of control.
You could barely even see the house from the street.
But at this rate, why would you want to?

Wouldn't this alone make you upset? The things listed above are nothing compared to how bad it got in Genesis. The earth became a boiling pot of angry, murderous, adulterous, prideful people.

Something had to be done.

THE FLOOD

In God's righteous anger He decided to destroy the earth with a flood but planned to save a remnant of His creation upon a boat to start fresh once the floods resided. Out of all the people that walked upon the earth at that time . . . God planned to save a man named Noah and his family; eight in all. Next, God told Noah to take upon the ark seven of each kind of clean animal; male and female, as well as to take two of each kind of unclean animal; male and female. (Genesis 7:2).

Can you imagine what people said to Noah while building the ark? The world was so very new and God had made everything from scratch. Would God REALLY destroy it? Was He bluffing? Well, jumping back to Genesis 3, we see that God holds dear to His word.

Do not eat of the fruit.
You will die.
They ate and God kept His word.
Don't believe me? By this point they were long gone.

So, Noah listened to God and does as He commanded of him.

> *But God remembered Noah and all the wild animals and the livestock that were with him in the ark, and he sent a wind over the earth, and the waters receded. Now the springs of the deep and the floodgates of the heavens had been closed, and the rain had stopped falling from the sky. The water receded steadily from the earth. At the end of the hundred and fifty days the water had gone down, and on the seventeenth day of the seventh month the ark came to rest on the mountains of Ararat. Genesis 8:1-4 NIV*

After one year, the waters resided enough for Noah and his family to get out of the ark. (Genesis 8:13-14)

> *God: "Come out of the ark, you and your wife and your sons and their wives. Bring out every kind of living creature that is with you—the birds, the animals, and all the creatures that move along the ground—so they can multiply on the earth and be fruitful and increase in number on it." Genesis 8:15-17 NIV*

So, Noah did as God requested.
But, not just that . . .
He did something that'd never been recorded before.

Then Noah built an altar to the LORD and, taking some of all the clean animals and clean birds, he sacrificed burnt offerings on it. The LORD smelled the pleasing aroma and said in his heart: "Never again will I curse the ground because of man, even though every inclination of his heart is evil from childhood. And never again will I destroy all living creatures, as I have done.

As long as the earth endures, seedtime and harvest, cold and heat, summer and winter, day and night will never cease."

Then God blessed Noah and his sons, saying to them, "Be fruitful and increase in number and fill the earth. The fear and dread of you will fall upon all the beasts of the earth and all the birds of the air, upon every creature that moves along the ground, and upon all the fish of the sea; they are given into your hands. Everything that lives and moves will be food for you. Just as I gave you the green plants, I now give you everything." Genesis 8:20-9:3 NIV

Just as God blessed Adam and Eve in the Garden, so He also blessed Noah and his family—the living remnant of God's precious creation. It was through Noah and his family and their descendants that would carry on the responsibility to take care of the earth and make babies. Remember, the gift analogy? Yeah, so this was a pretty big deal.

So, what happens next?
Noah's son's families fill the earth.

Noah's grandchildren had names like Egypt and Canaan which countries were named after. It was during this time that places such as Assyria, Babylon, Gaza, Sodom, Gomorrah and many others were formed.

THE SUFFERING OF JOB

The book of Job covers the span of God's servant Job's life. His book is placed later in the Old Testament but is widely believed to have chronologically happened sometime in the timeline of Genesis. Either way, this guy had a difficult life and not the best of friends.

> *In the land of Uz there lived a man whose name was Job. This man was blameless and upright; he feared God and shunned evil. He had seven sons and three daughters, and he owned seven thousand sheep, three thousand camels, five hundred yoke of oxen and five hundred donkeys, and had a large number of servants. He was the greatest man among all the people of the East. Job 1:1-3 NIV*

One day the council of angels came before the Lord and Satan joined them.

Side Note: Angels are not some puffy cherubs playing harps in the clouds all day like you see on Christmas cards. The Scriptures declare that angels are powerful (Matthew 26:53).

> *God: "Where have you come from?"*
>
> *Satan: "From roaming throughout the earth, going back and forth on it."*
>
> *God: "Have you considered my servant Job? There is no one on earth like him; he is blameless and upright, a man who fears God and shuns evil."*
>
> *Satan: "Does Job fear God for nothing? Have you not put a hedge around him and his household and everything he has? You have blessed the work of his hands, so that his flocks and herds are*

spread throughout the land. But now stretch out your hand and strike everything he has, and he will surely curse you to your face."

God: *"Very well, then, everything he has is in your power, but on the man himself do not lay a finger." Job 1:6-12 NIV*

Satan left God's presence and went to test Job. Job had a large family, a large amount of animals and hired servants. He had everything a man would want for his family and then some more. But Satan wanted to show God up and let Him know that He was only worshiped because He took care of His people.

So Satan took everything away from Job. In the course of one day, he lost his oxen and donkeys; next his sheep, camels and hired servants; then his sons and daughters were killed as a great wind struck the house they were in. Job tore his clothes and shaved his head. But even then Job did not curse the Lord but bowed down and worshiped Him.

But Satan still wasn't pleased. He demanded God to curse Job with painful sores head to toe. Job's wife had enough of the trials and told Job to curse God and die. Yet even then Job held his respect for the Lord.

The story continues as Job sits in silence and three of his friends, Eliphaz, Bildad and Zophar showed up and just sat with him. Finally, after seven days, Job broke the silence cursing his life.

Why was I even born!?

In the midst of the trial, Job's friends tried to explain away Job's problem as if he was being punished. Oh what Job would have given to understand what was going on in the heavenly realm.

In all of this, Job never renounced God but tried to find Him to get an explanation of what was happening in his life. Another guy named Elihu popped in to tell Job he shouldn't question his fate—that God's ways are far beyond our own.

After thirty-eight chapters of Job wondering, God spoke to Job.

> *Who is this that obscures my plans with words without knowledge? Brace yourself like a man; I will question you, and you shall answer me. Where were you when I laid the earth's foundation? Tell me, if you understand. Job 38:2-4 NIV*

Over the span of the next four chapters God enlightens Job of His power and breadth of His wonders. From creation to order, God explains to Job that there's more that goes on to keep order in the world than he might assume. His ways are much higher and mightier than the ways of man.

> *God: "Will the one who contends with the Almighty correct him? Let him who accuses God answer him!"*
>
> *Job: "I know that you can do all things; no purpose of yours can be thwarted. You asked, 'Who is this that obscures my plans without knowledge?' Surely I spoke of things I did not understand, things too wonderful for me to know. You said, 'Listen now, and I will speak; I will question you, and you shall answer me.' My ears had heard of you but now my eyes have seen you. Therefore I despise myself and repent in dust and ashes." Job 40:2; 42:2-6 NIV*

After speaking with Job, the Lord went to Eliphaz and told him of His anger for how he, Bildad and Zophar spoke of Him to Job. *You have not spoken truth about me! But, Job has. Go make a sacrifice to me. Job will pray for you and I will accept his prayer and not deal with you in the manner you deserve.* So the men did as the Lord had commanded.

The Lord blessed Job for his dedication through the trials that Satan had thrown at him. He restored Job's fortunes and gave him double what he had before. After this, Job lived another hundred and forty years and died full of years.

TOWER OF BABEL

Man remembered what it was like for Adam and Eve to speak to God face to face in the Garden and they wanted to have that same ability. People moved from miles around to this city to make a name for themselves and not be scattered across the world. To be scattered was dangerous. To be united meant a gathering of means.

So, what did they do?
They decided to build something massive.
They decided to build a tall tower.
They wanted to make a name for themselves.
They wanted to be with God.

(How silly does that sound today where we can send spaceships into outer space and obviously not reach the Heavens; it's outside of our capability. It's just not possible.)

The next part is interesting.
They did this lest they would be scattered across the earth.
Well, guess what happened next.
They built the tower.
But, they didn't reach the heavens.

Now, this angered God.

> But the Lord came down to see the city and the tower the people were building.

So, they got the presence of God, but not in the way they had expected it.

> God: "If as one people speaking the same language they have begun to do this, then nothing they plan to do will be impossible for them. Come, let us go down and confuse their language so they will not understand each other."

> So the Lord scattered them from there over all the earth, and they stopped building the city. That is why it was called Babel—because there the Lord confused the language of the whole world. From there the Lord scattered them over the face of the whole earth. Genesis 11:5-9 NIV

So, the people's plan was to build a great tower to make a great name for them and the result would be that they would not be scattered across the earth but be united.

But, God's plan for the people was to take care of the earth and make babies.

These two plans didn't line up very well. And, of course, God's plan won. Humanity, in a sense, wanted to become their own god. They wanted a name. They wanted the heavenly position. So, God protected them by confusing their language. This place in scripture is where we get the various people groups and their languages on the earth. Once God scrambled the languages of the people, they huddled into their own people groups and scattered across the earth.

God's people kept finding themselves in trouble. Anytime they listened to themselves instead of God, something went wrong. The people needed someone strong to follow. They needed a leader.

Now, onto that leader.

PART TWO
Family Figures

ABRAHAM & SARAH

CHAPTER THREE

I will make you into a great nation, and I will bless you; I will make your name great, and you will be a blessing.
Genesis 12:2 NIV

Recently, my wife and I purchased our first home! We were excited and thinking about all of the things that we could touch up and renovate in our (new to us) house. We had visited some friends not too long before who had gotten an artist to capture each of their houses that they'd lived in on canvas. They placed them on the wall in their entry way and we thought that was such a great idea. Then this idea occurred: What if we got the blueprint for our house and framed it. We didn't get to build our first house, but to see the original plans for the house hung up would be pretty nice!

After much rebellion and chaos on the earth, God had a plan. God figuratively laid out his blueprint for the universe on that great big table in the sky and called a new man and his wife to carry out that plan.

> The Lord had said to Abram, "Go from your country, your people and your father's household to the land I will show you.
>
> I will make you into a great nation,
> and I will bless you;
> I will make your name great,
> and you will be a blessing.
> I will bless those who bless you,
> and whoever curses you I will curse;
> and all peoples on earth
> will be blessed through you."

This is very important.
God blesses Abram and Sarai.
He gives them the same gift that He gave Adam and Eve.
But, there was a problem.
Abram and Sarai couldn't have children.
Was this some sort of sick joke?
What was God doing here?

> So Abram went, as the Lord had told him. Abram was seventy-five years old when he set out from Harran. He took his wife Sarai, his nephew Lot, all the possessions they had accumulated and the people they had acquired in Harran, and they set out for the land of Canaan, and they arrived there. The Lord appeared to Abram and said, "To your offspring I will give this land." So he built an altar there to the Lord, who had appeared to him. Genesis 12:1-5;7 NIV

Seventy-five years old.
Can you imagine this?
At this age, Abram had his life together.

or so he thought
He owned his own land.
He owned his own house.
He had his own hired workers.
Life was probably pretty great.

Abram was old when God called him and his wife. During our current age, at seventy-five years old, a person would be several years past retirement. But, this seems to be when Abram and Sarai's lives started to gain true meaning.

THE LORDS COVENANT

God: "Do not be afraid, Abram. I am your shield, your very great reward."

Abram: "Sovereign Lord, what can you give me since I remain childless?"

God: "Look up at the sky and count the stars—if indeed you can count them. So shall your offspring be." Genesis 15:1-2, 5 NIV

The scripture goes on to say that Abram believed God and God credited it to him as righteousness. Wow.

HAGAR AND ISHMAEL

Now Sarai, Abram's wife, had borne him no children. But she had an Egyptian slave named Hagar; so she said to Abram, "The Lord has kept me from having children. Go, sleep with my slave; perhaps I can build a family through her."

> *Abram agreed to what Sarai said. So after Abram had been living in Canaan ten years, Sarai his wife took her Egyptian slave Hagar and gave her to her husband to be his wife. He slept with Hagar, and she conceived. Genesis 16:1-4 NIV*

Wait. What just happened?
God had just laid everything out for them.
Let's take into account the struggle.
Sarai believed she could never bear children.
Now, she and her husband were told they'd have children.

That's a pretty heavy concept to hold on to when you're infertile.

Now, you may be reading this and know the end of the story.

But, Abram and Sarai did not.
They had to trust God and carry on.
So, they chose their slave Hagar to carry their child.
Now, as you can imagine . . . it just wasn't that simple.
Hagar in her childbearing came to despise Sarai.

Can you imagine being Hagar? She handled the duties of the house for Abram and Sarai and then her job description changed in an instant. No longer was she only to scrub the floors and feed the flocks, but she was to do the dirty work of carrying a child for her boss. How filthy do you think that made her feel? So, of course, when the pains of being pregnant began to sit in Hagar began to greatly despise Sarai.

> *Then Sarai said to Abram, "You are responsible for the wrong I am suffering. I put my slave in your*

arms, and now that she knows she is pregnant, she despises me."

"Your slave is in your hands," Abram said. "Do with her whatever you think best." Then Sarai mistreated Hagar; so she fled from her.

The angel of the Lord found Hagar near a spring in the desert.

Angel: "Hagar, slave of Sarai, where have you come from, and where are you going?"

Hagar: "I'm running away from my mistress Sarai."

Angel: "Go back to your mistress and submit to her." The angel added, "I will increase your descendants so much that they will be too numerous to count.

You are now pregnant and you will give birth to a son. You shall name him Ishmael, for the Lord has heard of your misery."

Hagar: "You are the God who sees me, for she said, 'I have now seen the One who sees me.'" Genesis 16:5-11;13 NIV

COVENANT

When Abram was ninety-nine years old, the Lord appeared to him and said, "I am God Almighty; walk before me faithfully and be blameless. Then I will make my covenant between me and you and will greatly increase your numbers."

Abram fell facedown, and God said to him, "As for me, this is my covenant with you: You will be the father of many nations. No longer will you be called

Abram; your name will be Abraham, for I have made you a father of many nations. I will make you very fruitful; I will make nations of you, and kings will come from you. I will establish my covenant as an everlasting covenant between me and you and your descendants after you for the generations to come, to be your God and the God of your descendants after you. The whole land of Canaan, where you now reside as a foreigner, I will give as an everlasting possession to you and your descendants after you; and I will be their God." Genesis 17:1-8 NIV

Now the Lord was gracious to Sarah as he had said, and the Lord did for Sarah what he had promised. Sarah became pregnant and bore a son to Abraham in his old age. At the very time God had promised him. Abraham gave the name Isaac to the son Sarah bore him. When his son Isaac was eight days old, Abraham circumcised him, as God commanded him. Abraham was a hundred years old when his son Isaac was born to him. Sarah said, "God has brought me laughter, and everyone who hears about this will laugh with me." And she added, "Who would have said to Abraham that Sarah would nurse children? Yet I have borne him a son in his old age." Genesis 21:1-7 NIV

(Apparently, even in biblical times, women weren't exactly truthful about their age. *God has brought me laughter . . . I have borne him a son in his old age.* Abram was 100 and Sarah was 90. Come on Sarah . . . you were up there, too!)

God keeps His promises.
Sometimes it's easier to go our own way.
But, it's important to let God do His thing.

ABRAHAM TESTED

> *Sometime later God tested Abraham. He said to him, "Abraham! . . . Take your son, your only son, whom you love—Isaac—and go to the region of Moriah. Sacrifice him there as a burnt offering on a mountain I will show you." Genesis 22:1-2 NIV*

Hold on.
God finally gave this family a child.
And now He wants them to sacrifice this child?
And when did the name change happen?
God changed their names to Abraham and Sarah.

> *Early the next morning Abraham got up and loaded his donkey. He took with him two of his servants and his son Isaac. When he had cut enough wood for the burnt offering, he set out for the place God had told him about.*

. . . Abraham was actually going to go through with it!

> *On the third day Abraham looked up and saw the place in the distance. He said to his servants, "Stay here with the donkey while I and the boy go over there. We will worship and then we will come back to you." Genesis 22:3-5 NIV*

At that point Abraham hadn't followed God for very long. Abraham was raised in Ur, which is in modern Iraq. In that society, people worshiped the moon and other gods. In their culture the moon god, Nanna, was the source of fertility for crops, herds and families.

What do people do when they want something?
They try to appeal to the bearer of that something.

The people would offer sacrifices to appeal to the "god". If nothing happened they would assume their gift wasn't enough, and they would then sacrifice even more. If they received what they wanted (in this case fertility), they knew their gift was accepted. THEN, they would give another gift out of gratitude (sounds exhausting!). The greatest sacrifice anyone could give was their firstborn— their heir. This told the gods that you meant business.

To Abraham, sacrifice was a part of life.
This was his "normal."
His wife was barren.
You have to know they begged "the gods" for a child.

But, God gave them a child.
And now He wants to take it?

> Abraham took the wood for the burnt offering and placed it on his son Isaac, and he himself carried the fire and the knife. As the two of them went on together, Isaac spoke up and said to his father Abraham, "Father?"
>
> "Yes, my son?" Abraham replied.
>
> "The fire and wood are here," Isaac said, "but where is the lamb for the burnt offering?"

(Uh oh)

> Abraham answered, "God himself will provide the lamb for the burnt offering, my son." And the two of them went on together.
>
> He bound his son Isaac and laid him on the altar, on top of the wood. Then he reached out his hand and took the knife to slay his son.

(Can you feel the tension rising?)

> *But the angel of the Lord called out to him from heaven:*
>
> *"Abraham! Abraham!"*
>
> *"Here I am," Abraham replied.*
>
> *"Do not lay a hand on the boy," he said.*
>
> *"Do not do anything to him. Now I know that you fear God, because you have not withheld from me your son, your only son."*

BLESSINGS

> *Abraham looked up and there in a thicket he saw a ram caught by its horns. He went over and took the ram and sacrificed it as a burnt offering instead of his son. So Abraham called that place 'The Lord Will Provide.'*
>
> *The angel of the Lord called to Abraham from heaven a second time and said, "I swear by myself, declares the Lord, that because you have done this and have not withheld your son, your only son, I will surely bless you." Genesis 22:6-17 NIV*

✳ God is different from the "gods" of Abraham's past.
The "gods" demanded exhaustive sacrifices.
Our God takes care of the sacrifice.

Now, here's to hoping that Isaac's childhood experience didn't give him daddy issues.

ISAAC & REBEKAH

CHAPTER FOUR

Two nations are in your womb, and two peoples from within you will be separated; one people will be stronger than the other, and the older will serve the younger. Genesis 25:23 NIV

In the ancient Middle East, your tribe was your family. We just read about how Abraham and Sarah left everything they ever knew to follow God's great plan for their new tribe. The interesting thing though, their tribe was quite small. At this point it was Abraham, Sarah, Isaac and a handful of other family and hired servants. Abraham and Sarah were getting older in age and Isaac was unmarried and childless.

THAT ESCALATED QUICKLY

Abraham was now very old, and the Lord had blessed him in every way. He said to the senior servant in his household, the one in charge of all that he had, "Put your hand under my thigh. I want you to swear by the Lord, the God of heaven and the God of earth, that you will not get a wife for my son from the daughters of the Canaanites, among whom I am living, but will go to my country and my own relatives and get a wife for my son Isaac."

Then the servant left . . . he prayed, "Lord, God of my master Abraham, make me successful today, and show kindness to my master Abraham. See, I am standing beside this spring, and the daughters of the townspeople are coming out to draw water. May it be that when I say to a young woman, 'Please let down your jar that I may have a drink,' and she says, 'Drink, and I'll water your camels too'—let her be the one you have chosen for your servant Isaac. By this I will know that you have shown kindness to my master."

Before he had finished praying, Rebekah came out with her jar on her shoulder . . . She went down to the spring, filled her jar and came up again.

The servant hurried to meet her and said, "Please give me a little water from your jar."

"Drink, my lord," she said, and quickly lowered the jar to her hands and gave him a drink. "I'll draw water for your camels too, until they have had enough to drink." Genesis 24:1-6, 10-19 NIV

Could this be the one?
He had one question.
Was she family?

Then he asked, "Whose daughter are you? Please tell me, is there room in your father's house for us to spend the night?"

> *She answered him, "I am the daughter of Bethuel, the son that Milkah bore to Nahor (Abraham's brother)." And she added, "We have plenty of straw and fodder, as well as room for you to spend the night."*
>
> *Then the man bowed down and worshiped the Lord, saying, "Praise be to the Lord, the God of my master Abraham, who has not abandoned his kindness and faithfulness to my master." Genesis 24:23-27 NIV*

After this, Abraham's servant met Rebekah's father and told him all about his journey and how God's hand was in on it all.

> *Laban and Bethuel answered, "This is from the Lord; we can say nothing to you one way or the other. Here is Rebekah; take her and go, and let her become the wife of your master's son, as the Lord has directed."*
>
> *When Abraham's servant heard what they said, he bowed down to the ground before the Lord.*
>
> *So they called Rebekah and asked her, "Will you go with this man?"*
>
> *"I will go," she said.*
>
> *So they sent their sister Rebekah on her way, along with her nurse and Abraham's servant and his men. And they blessed Rebekah and said to her, "Our sister, may you increase to thousands upon thousands; may your offspring possess the cities of their enemies." Genesis 24:50-60 NIV*

Can you imagine all of this playing out in front of you? All of this is happening and I did not read one sentence that told me Isaac was in on any of this. Now, this was a totally different culture of course.

Here's a father who has been promised great blessings in his life to inherit an incredible nation that would come from his literal lineage. Shortly before his death he pleads with his servant to be sure his son marries a righteous woman to carry on this ancestry of a royal nation. His servant goes to Abraham's native homeland to find this woman who no one even had a name for yet. He prays to God for the woman to carry out a specific conversation with him to be sure this was the right woman and it's her! Not only is it "her" but her family is all in because God was behind it.

Now, take a step back.
Do you remember where Abraham came from?
These people didn't worship Abraham's God.
They worshipped the gods of Abram's past.
They didn't have any skin in the game.
They could have easily said, "no way!"

But Abraham told his servant something important in Genesis 24:7. God was sending his angel before Abraham's servant. God was preparing the way the entire time. God led the woman to the servant just as much as he led the servant to the woman. Isaac was special, but so was Rebekah. God had a plan for these two. It was the continued plan that he gave to Abraham and Sarah: Take care of this place and make babies.

BIRTH PAINS

Just like his father and mother before him, Isaac and Rebekah began to have trouble trying to conceive.

Isaac prayed to the Lord on behalf of his wife, because she was childless. The Lord answered his prayer, and his wife Rebekah became pregnant. The babies jostled each other within her, and she said, "Why is this happening to me?" So she went to inquire of the Lord.

The Lord said to her: "Two nations are in your womb, and two peoples from within you will be separated; one people will be stronger than the other, and the older will serve the younger."

When the time came for her to give birth, there were twin boys in her womb. The first to come out was red, and his whole body was like a hairy garment; so they named him Esau. After this, his brother came out, with his hand grasping Esau's heel; so he was named Jacob. Isaac was sixty years old when Rebekah gave birth to them.

BIRTHRIGHT (AKA INHERITANCE)

The boys grew up, and Esau became a skillful hunter, a man of the open country, while Jacob was content to stay at home among the tents. Isaac, who had a taste for wild game, loved Esau, but Rebekah loved Jacob.

Once when Jacob was cooking some stew, Esau came in from the open country, famished. He said to Jacob, "Quick, let me have some of that red stew! I'm famished!"

Jacob replied, "First sell me your birthright."

"Look, I am about to die," Esau said. "What good is the birthright to me?"

But Jacob said, "Swear to me first." So he swore an oath to him, selling his birthright to Jacob.

Then Jacob gave Esau some bread and some lentil stew. He ate and drank, and then got up and left. So Esau despised his birthright. Genesis 25:21-34 NIV

FAMINE!

Now there was a famine in the land—besides the previous famine in Abraham's time—and Isaac went to Abimelek king of the Philistines in Gerar. The Lord appeared to Isaac and said, "Do not go down to Egypt; live in the land where I tell you to live. Stay in this land for a while, and I will be with you and will bless you. For to you and your descendants I will give all these lands and will confirm the oath I swore to your father Abraham. I will make your descendants as numerous as the stars in the sky and will give them all these lands, and through your offspring all nations on earth will be blessed, because Abraham obeyed me and did everything I required of him, keeping my commands, my decrees and my instructions." So Isaac stayed in Gerar. Genesis 26:1-6 NIV

Now, this part in scripture might seem out of place. Especially being that the stories on either side of this seem to flow as one piece. But, this short story helps us understand something that has yet to happen. One, there is a famine happening in the land which makes that stew story hold a ton more weight. Second, and more importantly, God wants this tribe to stay in the land that he has gifted them. *(Keep remembering the gift! It's the glue that holds all of these stories together).*

BLESSING (AKA GOD'S GIFT)

When Isaac was old and his eyes were so weak that he could no longer see, he called for Esau his older son and said to him,

> *"My son . . . I am now an old man and don't know the day of my death. Now then, get your equipment—your quiver and bow—and go out to the open country to hunt some wild game for me. Prepare me the kind of tasty food I like and bring it to me to eat, so that I may give you my blessing before I die." Genesis 27:1-4 NIV*

Rebekah overheard and told Jacob to do it so that he would have both the birthright and blessing! So, Jacob remembered that his brother was a hairy man and there was no way that his father would believe he was Esau if his father touched him. Long story short, Rebekah covered Jacob's arms and neck with goatskins and cooked up a nice meal for Isaac from two of the goats they had in the backyard.

> *Then he said, "My son, bring me some of your game to eat, so that I may give you my blessing." Jacob brought it to him and he ate; and he brought some wine and he drank. Then his father Isaac said to him, "Come here, my son, and kiss me." So he went to him and kissed him. When Isaac caught the smell of his clothes, he blessed him and said, "Ah, the smell of my son is like the smell of a field that the Lord has blessed. May God give you heaven's dew and earth's richness—an abundance of grain and new wine. May nations serve you and peoples bow down to you. Be lord over your brothers, and may the sons of your mother bow down to you. May those who curse you be cursed and those who bless you be blessed." Genesis 27:25-29 NIV*

In the ancient world, blessings were a pretty big deal. If you were the firstborn son . . . life went pretty well for you (unless you royally screwed up). The firstborn son received a double portion of the inheritance as well as the blessing of the family. In other words, you would become the head of your extended family and its lineage would be carried on through you.

RUN, RUN FAR AWAY

After Isaac finished blessing him, and Jacob had scarcely left his father's presence, his brother Esau came in from hunting. He too prepared some tasty food and brought it to his father. Then he said to him, "My father, please sit up and eat some of my game, so that you may give me your blessing."

His father Isaac asked him, "Who are you?" "I am your son," he answered, "your firstborn, Esau." Isaac trembled violently and said, "Who was it, then, that hunted game and brought it to me? I ate it just before you came and I blessed him—and indeed he will be blessed!" When Esau heard his father's words, he burst out with a loud and bitter cry and said to his father, "Bless me—me too, my father!" But he said, "Your brother came deceitfully and took your blessing." Esau said, "Isn't he rightly named Jacob? This is the second time he has taken advantage of me: He took my birthright, and now he's taken my blessing!" Then he asked, "Haven't you reserved any blessing for me?" Isaac answered Esau, "I have made him lord over you and have made all his relatives his servants, and I have sustained him with grain and new wine. So what can I possibly do for you, my son?" Esau said to his father, "Do you have only one blessing, my father? Bless me too, my father!" Then Esau wept aloud.

His father Isaac answered him, "Your dwelling will be away from the earth's richness, away from the dew of heaven above. You will live by the sword and you will serve your brother. But when you grow restless, you will throw his yoke

from off your neck." Esau held a grudge against Jacob because of the blessing his father had given him. He said to himself, "The days of mourning for my father are near; then I will kill my brother Jacob."

When Rebekah was told what her older son Esau had said, she sent for her younger son Jacob and said to him, "Your brother Esau is planning to avenge himself by killing you. Now then, my son, do what I say: Flee at once to my brother Laban in Harran." Genesis 27:30-40 NIV

Harran. We just keep coming back to this place! Jacob fled back to the land that his grandfather Abraham had once lived and where his mother grew up before marrying his father. Just so we're in the same place, this is not the land promised to Jacob—the gift. It's interesting that Isaac blessed Jacob and soon after, because of his deceitfulness, left the land and the people that was the blessing.

Now, onto Harran!

JACOB & RACHEL

CHAPTER FIVE

All peoples on earth will be blessed through you and your offspring. I am with you and will watch over you wherever you go. Genesis 28:14-15 NIV

Let's take a second and recapture what's going on. Isaac and Rebekah got pregnant and had twin boys, Jacob and Esau. Esau was the oldest who was rightly deserving of firstborn son privileges: birthright and double inheritance. Jacob, along with his mother, tricked Isaac into handing over both birthright and inheritance. After the trickery was over, Jacob fled for his life to Harran.

Camera.
Set.
Action.

JACOB'S DREAM

Jacob left Beersheba and set out for Harran. When he reached a certain place, he stopped for the night because the sun had set. Taking one of the stones there, he put it under his head and lay down to sleep.

He had a dream in which he saw a stairway resting on the earth, with its top reaching to heaven, and the angels of God were ascending and descending on it. There above it stood the Lord, and he said: "I am the Lord, the God of your father Abraham and the God of Isaac. I will give you and your descendants the land on which you are lying. Your descendants will be like the dust of the earth, and you will spread out to the west and to the east, to the north and to the south. All peoples on earth will be blessed through you and your offspring. I am with you and will watch over you wherever you go, and I will bring you back to this land. I will not leave you until I have done what I have promised you." Genesis 28:10-15 NIV

Interesting isn't it?
Not only does Isaac *unknowingly* give Jacob the gift.
God then, based on Isaac's gifting, fulfills that gift.

When Jacob awoke from his sleep, he thought, "Surely the Lord is in this place, and I was not aware of it." He was afraid and said, "How awesome is this place! This is none other than the house of God; this is the gate of heaven."

Early the next morning Jacob took the stone he had placed under his head and set it up as a pillar and poured oil on top of it. He called that place Bethel, though the city used to be called Luz.

Then Jacob made a vow, saying, "If God will be with me and will watch over me on this journey I am taking and will give me food to eat and clothes to wear so that I return safely to my father's household, then the Lord will be my God and this stone that I have set up as a pillar will be God's house, and of all that you give me I will give you a tenth."
Genesis 28:16-22 NIV

BACK TO HARRAN, THE LAND OF ENCHANTMENT

Then Jacob continued on his journey and came to the land of the eastern peoples. There he saw a well in the open country, with three flocks of sheep lying near it because the flocks were watered from that well. The stone over the mouth of the well was large. When all the flocks were gathered there, the shepherds would roll the stone away from the well's mouth and water the sheep. Then they would return the stone to its place over the mouth of the well.

Jacob: "My brothers, where are you from?"

Shepherds: "We're from Harran,"

Jacob: "Do you know Laban, Nahor's grandson?"

Shepherds: "Yes, we know him,"

Jacob: "Is he well?"

Shepherds: "Yes, he is, and here comes his daughter Rachel with the sheep."

Shepherd: "Look, the sun is still high; it is not time for the flocks to be gathered. Water the sheep and take them back to pasture."

> *Shepherds: "We can't! When all the flocks are gathered and we have help to roll the stone away from the mouth of the well. Then we will water the sheep."*
>
> *While he was still talking with them, Rachel came with her father's sheep, for she was a shepherd. When Jacob saw Rachel daughter of his uncle Laban, and Laban's sheep, he went over and rolled the stone away from the mouth of the well and watered his uncle's sheep. Genesis 29:1-10 NIV*

Did you catch that?

The stone was large enough that the shepherds needed backup.

Jacob manhandles the stone and shows off in front of Rachel.

As if that's not enough for a first interaction, read on...

> *Then Jacob kissed Rachel and began to weep aloud. He told Rachel that he was a relative of her father and a son of Rebekah. So she ran and told her father. As soon as Laban heard the news about Jacob, his sister's son, he hurried to meet him. He embraced him and kissed him and brought him to his home, and there Jacob told him all these things. Then Laban said to him, "You are my own flesh and blood." Genesis 29:11-14 NIV*

Let's take a step back for a second. Earlier when we read the love story of Isaac and Rebekah we walked with Abraham's hired servant as he trekked to Harran to find Isaac a wife. We cheered with him as he greeted Abraham's family and met Rebekah. We heard him share with everyone that God was a part of the entire journey. Nothing had been done without God's help. As we read this story of Jacob meeting his bride-to-be, the encounter is told through Jacob's actions and not his words. But even so, God directed Jacob to the well.

SISTER WIVES

> *After Jacob had stayed with him for a whole month, Laban said to him, "Just because you are a relative of mine, should you work for me for nothing? Tell me what your wages should be." Genesis 29:14-15 NIV*

Of course, Jacob was already head over heels for Rachel. So Jacob tells Laban,

> *"I'll work for you seven years in return for your younger daughter Rachel" Genesis 29:18 NIV*

That's one lovesick dude.

Laban quickly agreed to the terms. He thought it was better to marry her off to someone familiar than to someone from outside the tribe. So Jacob went off to work. It didn't feel very long for lovesick Jacob before those seven years were up and he was quick to remember the agreement. Jacob ran to Laban and said,

> *"Give me my wife; I've completed what we agreed I'd do. I'm ready to consummate my marriage"*

(I think my father-in-law would've fainted if I walked up to him and said I was in a hurry to consummate my marriage . . . but hey, seven years is a long time.)

> *Laban invited everyone around and threw a big feast. At evening, though, he got his daughter Leah and brought her to the marriage bed, and Jacob slept with her. Genesis 29:21-24 MSG*

Wow!
What a shot!
I would be livid.

When morning came, Jacob realized that it was in fact Leah and not Rachel in bed with him . . . he married the wrong sister!

So what does Jacob do? What any of us would do. He confronted Laban and asked what was this all about! And Laban's answer was a bit of a cheap shot . . . *We don't do it that way in our country. We don't marry off the younger daughter before the older. Enjoy your week of honeymoon, and then we'll give you the other one also* . . . The cost, you ask? Yes, you guessed it, another seven years.

Lovesick Jacob agreed to the terms of course and worked another seven years for Laban. But this time Jacob got the woman prior to the work. After the honeymoon week was over, Laban handed off his daughter Rachel to be married to Jacob and they consummated their marriage.

The next part in scripture is very quick to state that Jacob loved Rachel more than Leah. To be fair, Jacob was in love at first sight when he saw Rachel for the first time. But God remembered Leah.

> *When God realized that Leah was unloved, he opened her womb. But Rachel was barren.*

Leah became pregnant and had a son. She named him Reuben "This is a sign," she said, "that God has seen my misery; and a sign that now my husband will love me."

She became pregnant again and had another son. "God heard," she said, "that I was unloved and so he gave me this son also." She named this one Simeon (God-Heard).

She became pregnant yet again—another son. She said, "Now maybe my husband will connect with me—I've given him three sons!" That's why she named him Levi (Connect).

She became pregnant a final time and had a fourth son. She said, "This time I'll praise God." So she named him Judah (Praise-God). Then she stopped having children. Genesis 29:31-35 MSG

Leah doesn't get very much attention in the Bible from the writer, from her father or from her husband. Her father named her Leah, which literally means 'dull'. She was unloved by many from the day she was born. That. Is. Heartbreaking.

Patrick Mead says it best when he says, "our hearts need to break for Leah." This is a woman who helped the father of nations be a father in the first place. The greatest sign of love she was ever shown was God opening her womb. Even in that she was still so blindsided by wanting love and affection from her husband.

People often focus on 'poor Jacob' for not getting to marry Rachel right away and we look over how Leah had to marry a man (we don't even know if she loved him when they got married) and she knew from the beginning that he loved her younger, prettier sister. Can you imagine already feeling so unloved and your father forces you into tricking the man your sister loved into marrying you? I can only imagine how shameful and embarrassed Leah must have felt . . .

And then she went into this marriage and at least could give Jacob children but then (SPOILER ALERT) Rachel has two children AND THEY ARE HIS FAVORITES, TOO. What kind of cruel joke is that for her? Even her children aren't favored over Rachel's children. Second best daughter, second best, wife, second best mom . . . She lived her life coming second to the daughter born after her. There really is no better phrase for her than "our hearts need to break for Leah".

Leah spent her life trying to please Jacob. We finally see when she has Judah that she stops focusing her entire life on how she can please her husband and get him to pay attention to her and she finally decides to give glory to God. I can only hope that Leah found true happiness in her life by looking for God's approval and unconditional love.

JOSEPH'S BIRTH

But, life wasn't a piece of cake for Rachel either. She sat and watched as her sister continued to give her husband children for years without being able to contribute. She prayed for a child of her own, but she was barren. She even gave her female servant over to Jacob to have children just to feel as if they were her own. Then Leah did the same and had some more children naturally. I can imagine the tears. The late nights. The negative results month after month. But, then something changed.

JACOB & RACHEL

Then God remembered Rachel; he listened to her and enabled her to conceive. She became pregnant and gave birth to a son and said, "God has taken away my disgrace." She named him Joseph, and said, "May the Lord add to me another son." Genesis 30:22-24 NIV

Can you imagine?
Many girls dream from an early age of marriage.
Dreams of bearing children and raising a family.
After twenty years of marriage Rachel was able to conceive.

You can read in her own words that she felt disgrace.

My wife and I had been trying to conceive for months. The most difficult part of the waiting was watching my wife scroll through Facebook and finding out other friends of hers were pregnant. Each month we were greeted with a negative pregnancy test and tears as we watched others celebrate new life. Now, our story didn't go on as long as Rachel's did, but I can somewhat empathize with Jacob, as I know my wife can with Rachel.

Waiting. Was. Terrible.
All sorts of questions came to mind:

How long will it take?
Will we ever have children?
Am I infertile?
The questions go on.

But to read this story and to understand that God was behind Rachel's barrenness was heart wrenching.

You know the gift.
You know the promise.

Jacob was blessed with the land and was told to bear children. His family would be blessed with many generations . . . as many as the stars in the sky and the sand on the seashore.

So, what was going on?

The writer may be suggesting that Jacob's plans and God's plans were not one in the same. First, Jacob planned to marry Rachel but God planned for him to marry Leah. Second, Jacob planned to have children through Rachel to carry on the family name, yet her womb was barren and God opened up Leah's womb to bear children. From reading this story, we see a difference in God's plan versus Jacob's plan.

FLEE. DEATH. ARRIVE.

Next, you see Jacob and his family flee from Laban's home to head back to Canaan. Canaan, I remind you, is the land of promise. But this is also where his betrayed brother and father live (you know, the inheritance and blessing story).

JACOB PREPARES TO MEET ESAU. In their fleeing, Jacob remembers who he is returning to and sends messengers ahead of him to greet his brother.

> *He instructed them: "This is what you are to say to my lord Esau: 'Your servant Jacob says, I have been staying with Laban and have remained there till now. I have cattle and donkeys, sheep and goats,*

> *male and female servants. Now I am sending this message to my lord, that I may find favor in your eyes." Genesis 32:4-5 NIV*

When Jacob's messengers left, they saw Esau coming toward them four hundred men strong. Of course Jacob became filled with fear. So he split up his men into two groups thinking if one group was killed the other would survive. In great distress he began to pray to the Lord.

Jacob goes on to select a gift that he believes will surely win over the favor of his brother in his anger. Are you ready to hear what the gift was? Two hundred female goats, twenty male goats, two hundred ewes and twenty rams, thirty female camels with their young, forty cows and ten bulls, and twenty female donkeys and ten male donkeys. This guy is scared for his life! He tells his servants to ride ahead of him with the animals and when Esau sees them and asks to whom they belong to tell him that they are a gift from his brother Jacob and that he is coming behind them. Not only are the gifts sent ahead of him, Jacob also makes sure that each set of animals has their own servant bringing the herds individually to Esau so that he would be in awe each time a gift was presented to him. After sending the herds ahead, Jacob spent the night in the camp.

During the night Jacob took his family and his possessions and sent them across a stream ahead of him. Before he crossed over, a man came near and they wrestled until daybreak.

> *When the man saw that he could not overpower him, he touched the socket of Jacob's hip so that his hip was wrenched as he wrestled with the man. Then the man said, "Let me go, for it is daybreak."*

But Jacob replied, "I will not let you go unless you bless me." The man asked him, "What is your name?" "Jacob," he answered. Then the man said, "Your name will no longer be Jacob, but Israel, because you have struggled with God and with humans and have overcome."

Jacob said, "Please tell me your name."
But he replied, "Why do you ask my name?"

Then he blessed him there. So Jacob called the place Peniel, saying, "It is because I saw God face to face, and yet my life was spared." Genesis 32:25-30 NIV

This scene brings light to the continuous struggle Jacob has endured in his story. His story is characterized by searching for blessing. His story began with him stealing his brother's blessing and continues as he tries to live up to the standard of that blessing.

JACOB MEETS ESAU. But now it's time for Jacob to see his brother for the first time in twenty years. How was Esau going to react? What was he going to look like after all these years? Was he going to be wealthy or poor? Did he have sons and daughters? Was he going to be accepted back into the family? Can you imagine all of the thoughts pouring into Jacob's head?

Jacob went forward to meet his brother and bowed down to the ground seven times (seven in Hebrew meant something was complete). To Jacob's surprise, Esau came running and hugged him. Now, this wasn't just a hug . . . this was an embrace. The scriptures say that Esau threw his arms around Jacob's neck and kissed him.

Looking up, Esau asked who the women and children were with Jacob. Rachel, Leah and the female servants came forward with their children and greeted Esau. During the celebration and uniting of families, Esau pulled Jacob aside and asked him,

> "What's the meaning of all these flocks and herds I met?"
>
> "To find favor in your eyes, my lord," he said.
>
> But Esau said, "I already have plenty, my brother. Keep what you have for yourself." "No, please!" said Jacob. "If I have found favor in your eyes, accept this gift from me." Genesis 33:8-10 NIV

Esau accepted the gifts to satisfy his brother. Esau then asked Jacob to join him back on his journey home but Jacob insisted that he stay and journey at a slower pace for the sake of the herds and children.

Jacob led his family to another city near his brother called Shechem in Canaan (yes, the promised land). Jacob's family pitched their tents and built an altar to God.

DINAH AND THE SCHECHEMITES. The next scene is one like you might find on Game of Thrones. After settling in the city of Shechem, the man Shechem himself found the only daughter of Jacob desirable. So he took her and raped her. He fell in love with her and wanted to take her as his wife. So he asked his father to get the girl for him.

Jacob heard the news and took his sons along with him to bring light to the matter.

They.
Were.
Furious.

They met Shechem and his father Hamor outside of their home.

> *Hamor said to them, "My son Shechem has his heart set on your daughter. Please give her to him as his wife. Intermarry with us; give us your daughters and take our daughters for yourselves. You can settle among us; the land is open to you. Live in it, trade in it, and acquire property in it."*
>
> *Then Shechem said to Dinah's father and brothers, "Let me find favor in your eyes, and I will give you whatever you ask. Make the price for the bride and the gift I am to bring as great as you like, and I'll pay whatever you ask me. Only give me the young woman as my wife."*
>
> *Because their sister Dinah had been defiled, Jacob's sons replied deceitfully as they spoke to Shechem and his father Hamor. They said to them, "We can't do such a thing; we can't give our sister to a man who is not circumcised. That would be a disgrace to us. We will enter into an agreement with you on one condition only: that you become like us by circumcising all your males. Then we will give you our daughters and take your daughters for ourselves. We'll settle among you and become one people with you. But if you will not agree to be circumcised, we'll take our sister and go." Genesis 34:8-17 NIV*

The agreement was made. Hamor and Shechem went back to the men of the city and they were immediately circumcised! After three days of the men being sore from ... well, you know ... Jacob's sons, Simeon and Levi, killed all the males in the city and took Dinah home with them. Next, the sons of Jacob looted their city and seized their flocks, herds and donkeys. They... took... everything, even the women and children.

Jacob.
Was.
Livid.

> *"You have brought trouble on me by making me obnoxious to the Canaanites and Perizzites, the people living in this land. We are few in number, and if they join forces against me and attack me, I and my household will be destroyed."*
> *But they replied, "Should he have treated our sister like a prostitute?" Genesis 34:30-31 NIV*

BETHEL: BLESSING. Then God told Jacob to get up and go Bethel; build an altar and to settle there. This is the place where Jacob met God while fleeing from Esau at the beginning of this chapter.

Jacob rushed to tell his entire household and all that was with him to get rid of all the foreign gods and purify themselves; even to change their clothes! It was in that moment that God made clear that His people would be clean and set apart. Jacob had nearly allowed God's people to intermarry with those God was trying to keep them set apart from.

Remember Abraham pleading with his servant to find Isaac a wife from his own people? Marrying a Canaanite was not an option. They have their own gods and idols in which they worship, but God was trying to create a people group that would be an example to foreigners.

God cared for other nations, but He wanted his people to be *the influencers*, not *the influenced*.

Jacob rushed and set up a stone pillar where he and God spoke and pouring out a drink offering and oil on it, he called it Bethel.

DEATH. Wow, a lot has gone on in nine months. Can you imagine Rachel's pregnancy? Well, the time had come for Rachel to give birth but they were still on the road. She had great difficulty in giving birth and died. But as she breathed her last breath she named her son Ben-Oni, which Jacob later renamed him Benjamin. They buried her on the way to Ephrath (otherwise known as Bethlehem).

While on the road, they pitched tents and Rueben, the first born (you know, the one who gets the inheritance and blessing), went in and slept with his father's concubine Bilhah (Rachel's servant, AKA his brothers Dan and Naphtali's mom. Gross.) Interestingly, the scriptures don't tell us Jacob's feelings on the matter, but I'm sure we can think up some things. More on that later.

ARRIVE. Now, we watch as Jacob finally sets foot in the land of his father Isaac and grandfather Abraham. You'd expect celebration. But, what we find is a very old Isaac who soon breathed his last breath at the old age of one hundred and eighty years old. The scriptures say he was old and full of years.

While Jacob was off, we miss out on the story of Abraham, Sarah, Isaac, Rebekah and Esau during those years. But we do know Esau married women from Canaan (a big no-no). There were probably scenes, like that of a soap opera, of disapproval of Esau's marriage choices.

Now, onto that favorite son.

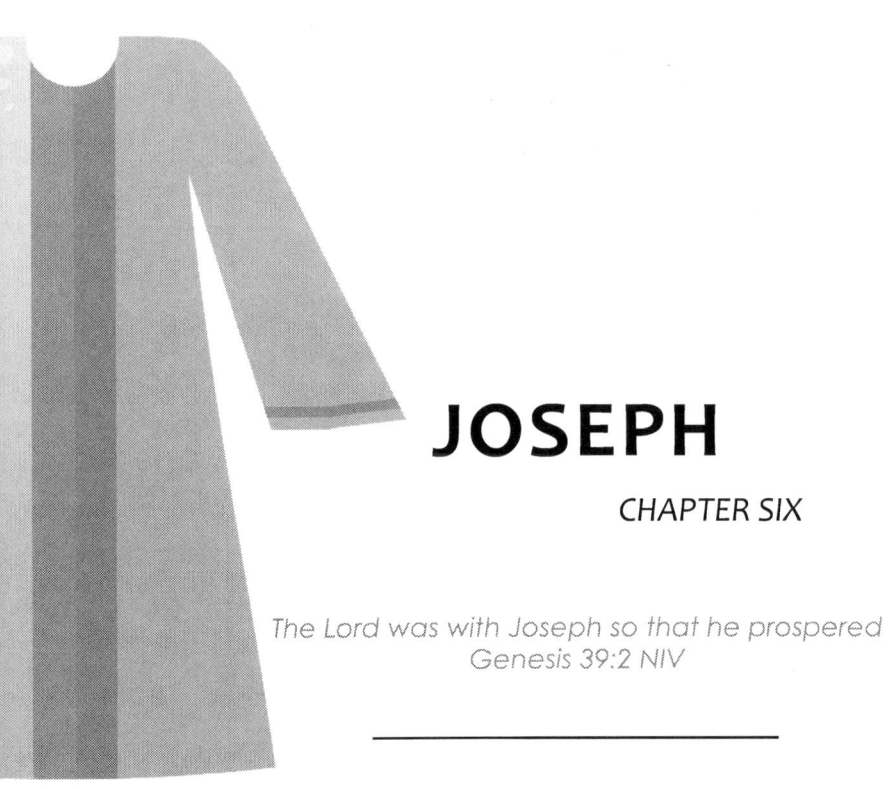

JOSEPH

CHAPTER SIX

The Lord was with Joseph so that he prospered
Genesis 39:2 NIV

COAT PART ONE

Jacob and his family had now settled in Canaan (AKA the Promised Land. AKA the Gift) Joseph, one of Jacob and Rachel's sons, was the most favored child. Now, this isn't just an assumption about the text . . . it literally reads:

> *Now Israel [Jacob] loved Joseph more than any of his other sons Genesis 37:3 NIV*

He loved Joseph so much that he had a special coat made for him to wear. This coat was ornate and visually described the preference Jacob had for Joseph. Apparently, the preference of Rachel over Leah lived on through the preferential treatment of Joseph. His brothers felt the disconnect between them and their father in comparison to Joseph and his relationship. The brothers hated Joseph because of this.

DREAMER PART ONE

Now, to make matters worse Joseph had a dream. This wasn't just any ordinary dream. This dream further exemplified that Joseph was favored over his brothers. So, Joseph kept the dream to himself . . .

No, of course not. He told his brothers the dream and they hated him even more!

> He said to them, "Listen to this dream I had: We were binding sheaves of grain out in the field when suddenly my sheaf rose and stood upright, while your sheaves gathered around mine and bowed down to it." His brothers said to him, "Do you intend to reign over us? Will you actually rule us?" And they hated him all the more because of his dream and what he had said.
>
> Then he had another dream, and he told it to his brothers. "Listen," he said, "I had another dream, and this time the sun and moon and eleven stars were bowing down to me."
>
> When he told his father as well as his brothers, his father rebuked him and said, "What is this dream you had? Will your mother and I and your brothers actually come and bow down to the ground before you?" His brothers were jealous of him, but his father kept the matter in mind. Genesis 37:6-11 NIV

PIT PART ONE

Joseph's brothers had gone out into the fields to work the flocks, and Jacob called Joseph to check on them and report back.

Joseph found his brothers and they saw him approaching. While a ways off, his brothers plotted to kill him. Can you feel the anger and jealousy? How deep the pain must be for the brothers to want to kill him. The brothers said to one another, *here comes that dreamer*... as he approached. Looking around, they planned to throw his corpse into an empty cistern and tell their father a ferocious animal had killed him.

But Reuben, the oldest brother, wanted to save his brother. He pleaded for them to leave Joseph in the cistern and not kill him (he planned to go back and rescue him later).

When Joseph arrived the brothers stripped him of his ornate robe and threw him into the cistern as planned.

PICNIC

But, of course, throwing your brother into a cistern can work up an appetite so they laid out in the grass and began to eat. You can almost hear Joseph yelling for help in the background while the brothers eat their meal before a caravan of Ishmaelites begin to drive by.

(Side note: Ishmael was Abraham's son through his servant Hagar; Sarah's surrogate per se. So... long lost family you might say.)

The caravan was on their way to Egypt but Judah, one of the brothers, spoke up and said:

> "What will we gain if we kill our brother and cover up his blood? Come, let's sell him to the Ishmaelites and not lay our hands on him; after all, he is our brother, our own flesh and blood." His brothers agreed.

(Phew!)

> So when the Midianite merchants came by, his brothers pulled Joseph up out of the cistern and sold him for twenty shekels of silver to the Ishmaelites, who took him to Egypt. Genesis 37:26-28 NIV

(Side note: Jesus was sold for 20 shekels of silver when his disciple Judas betrayed him. Hmm. Price of a slave apparently hadn't changed much in the two thousand years between Joseph's story and Jesus in the New Testament. That's nearly the same difference in time between Jesus' betrayal and today!)

> When Reuben returned to the cistern and saw that Joseph was not there, he tore his clothes. He went back to his brothers and said, "The boy isn't there! Where can I turn now?"
>
> Then they got Joseph's robe, slaughtered a goat and dipped the robe in the blood. They took the ornate robe back to their father and said, "We found this. Examine it to see whether it is your son's robe." Genesis 37:29-32 NIV

Of course Jacob recognized the robe!
Jacob LOVED Joseph.

He was the golden child.

> "It is my son's robe! Some ferocious animal has devoured him. Joseph has surely been torn to pieces."
>
> Then Jacob tore his clothes, put on sackcloth and mourned for his son many days. All his sons and daughters came to comfort him, but he refused to be comforted. "No," he said, "I will continue to mourn until I join my son in the grave." So his father wept for him. Genesis 37:33-35 NIV

The brothers thought after the "death" of their brother that maybe finally they would get the attention of their father in his mourning, but even then they felt rejected.

Next, the scene changes to Joseph on his journey with [his long lost family] the Ishmaelites. They sold Joseph in Egypt to Potiphar, one of Pharaoh's officials.

JUDAH AND TAMAR

Now, the scene abruptly changes again to a drastically different scenario in scripture. As Joseph was being sold off in Egypt, his brother Judah left home for a city called Adullam.

> There Judah met the daughter of a Canaanite man named Shua. He married her and made love to her; she became pregnant and gave birth to a son, who was named Er. She conceived again and gave birth to a son and named him Onan. She gave birth to still another son and named him Shelah. Genesis 38:2-5 NIV

Some time went by and Er, Judah's firstborn, was of age to marry. So, Judah found Tamar and married them off. But there was a problem—Er was wicked in the Lord's sight. So God put Er to death.

During this time period, it was normal for the second born son to take the wife of his older brother in their death. So, Judah requested this of Onan so that they could have children and carry on the family name. But, Onan didn't quite follow through with the request. Why? Well, Onan knew that this child would be considered Tamar and Er's child and not his own. He wanted his own family and not just provide offspring for his brother and sister-in-law. So, what happened next? God put Onan to death for his wickedness also.

Judah got smart and he told Tamar to live as a widow in her father's home and wait for Shelah to come of age to marry.

(But, Judah wasn't going to go through with it. He had already lost two sons and didn't want to lose his youngest.)

A while later, Judah's wife died and Tamar found out. She hurried to take off her widow's clothes and put on a veil to disguise herself. They ran into each other on the street and Judah believed she was a prostitute.

(Awkward.)

Not realizing who she was, he paid her to sleep with him. She became pregnant and word got back to Judah. But not in the way you might think. Judah heard that his daughter-in-law was guilty of prostitution and as a result was pregnant.

Bring her out and have her burned to death!

Tamar then sent a message to Judah explaining that he was the father. It was then that he realized what he had done.

> *When the time came for her to give birth, there were twin boys in her womb. As she was giving birth, one of them put out his hand; so the midwife took a scarlet thread and tied it on his wrist and said, "This one came out first." But when he drew back his hand, his brother came out, and she said, "So this is how you have broken out!" And he was named Perez. Then his brother, who had the scarlet thread on his wrist, came out. And he was named Zerah. Genesis 38:27-30 NIV*

First off, what just happened? We were trekking along the story of Joseph . . . we even started to kind of understand who he was . . . who took him and to where. And then it felt as if the movie reel had skipped to the next movie.

(When something in scripture seems out of place, take note of that something. It is probably important.)

Looking back at Genesis as a whole, the story of Judah has similarities along with Adam, Noah and Terah. These fathers each had three sons and two of their three died because of their wickedness.

In this story the same thing is happening. Judah's first and second born sons died due to their wickedness and Judah didn't want to lose the third one. This was his last chance at continuing his family name. Due to the righteousness of Tamar and God's faithfulness, Judah's family line was continued by Perez and Zerah. More on that later.

EGYPT

Now, taking up where we left off with Joseph. He arrived in Egypt with the Ishmaelite caravan where they sold him to an Egyptian man named Potiphar.

He was not your average Egyptian.
Potiphar was the high official to the Pharaoh of Egypt.

> *The Lord was with Joseph so that he prospered, and he lived in the house of his Egyptian master. When his master saw that the Lord was with him and that the Lord gave him success in everything he did Joseph found favor in his eyes and became his attendant. Potiphar put him in charge of his household, and he entrusted to his care everything he owned. From the time he put him in charge of his household and of all that he owned, the Lord blessed the household of the Egyptian because of Joseph. The blessing of the Lord was on everything Potiphar had, both in the house and in the field. So Potiphar left everything he had in Joseph's care; with Joseph in charge, he did not concern himself with anything except the food he ate. Genesis 39:2-6 NIV*

COAT PART TWO

> *Now Joseph was well-built and handsome, and after a while his master's wife took notice of Joseph and said, "Come to bed with me!" Genesis 39:7 NIV*

Okay. That just escalated quickly.

> *But he refused. "With me in charge," he told her, "my master does not concern himself with anything in the house; everything he owns he has entrusted to my care. No one is greater in this house than I am. My master has withheld nothing from me except you, because you are his wife. How then could I do such a wicked thing and sin against God?" Genesis 39:8-9 NIV*

This woman came to Joseph day after day and he continually refused her. Kudos to Joseph. The scriptures say he even refused to be with her ("This was not part of my job description!") Considering Potiphar's job and the amount of time he had to be out of the house to take care of his duties, his wife probably got pretty lonely. Joseph was in the right place at the wrong time.

> *One day he went into the house to attend to his duties, and none of the household servants was inside. She caught him by his cloak and said, "Come to bed with me!" But he left his cloak in her hand and ran out of the house. Genesis 39:11-12 NIV*

Cloak in her hand? Come on Joseph, you made it so easy for her. Potiphar's wife told her servants that Joseph took advantage of her and made a scandal of things.

Potiphar burned with anger.

After all that I've done for this boy? I've given him a job! I've taken care of him; Put him in charge of my entire household; Fed him and clothed him. This is how he repays me?

PIT PART TWO

After hearing the story from his wife, Potiphar threw Joseph in prison where all of the king's prisoners were kept. But of course, the charges were flawed and Joseph was innocent.

> But while Joseph was there in the prison, the Lord was with him; he showed him kindness and granted him favor in the eyes of the prison warden. So the warden put Joseph in charge of all those held in the prison, and he was made responsible for all that was done there. The warden paid no attention to anything under Joseph's care, because the Lord was with Joseph and gave him success in whatever he did. Genesis 39:20-23 NIV

DREAMER PART TWO

After Joseph had been in prison for some time, he gained two new prisoners in the section he was in charge of. One was a cupbearer of the king and the other was the king's baker.

> After they had been in custody for some time, each of the two men—the cupbearer and the baker of the king of Egypt, who were being held in prison—had a dream the same night, and each dream had a meaning of its own.
>
> When Joseph came to them the next morning, he saw that they were dejected. So he asked Pharaoh's officials who were in custody with him in his master's house, "Why do you look so sad today?"
>
> "We both had dreams," they answered, "but there is no one to interpret them."

Then Joseph said to them, "Do not interpretations belong to God? Tell me your dreams."

So the chief cupbearer told Joseph his dream. He said to him, "In my dream I saw a vine in front of me, and on the vine were three branches. As soon as it budded, it blossomed, and its clusters ripened into grapes. Pharaoh's cup was in my hand, and I took the grapes, squeezed them into Pharaoh's cup and put the cup in his hand."

"This is what it means," Joseph said to him. "The three branches are three days. Within three days Pharaoh will lift up your head and restore you to your position, and you will put Pharaoh's cup in his hand, just as you used to do when you were his cupbearer. But when all goes well with you, remember me and show me kindness; mention me to Pharaoh and get me out of this prison. I was forcibly carried off from the land of the Hebrews, and even here I have done nothing to deserve being put in a dungeon."

When the chief baker saw that Joseph had given a favorable interpretation, he said to Joseph, "I too had a dream: On my head were three baskets of bread. In the top basket were all kinds of baked goods for Pharaoh, but the birds were eating them out of the basket on my head."

"This is what it means," Joseph said. "The three baskets are three days. Within three days Pharaoh will lift off your head and impale your body on a pole. And the birds will eat away your flesh."

Now the third day was Pharaoh's birthday, and he gave a feast for all his officials. He lifted up the heads of the chief cupbearer and the chief baker in the presence of his officials: He restored the chief cupbearer to his position, so that he once again put the cup into Pharaoh's hand—but he impaled the chief baker, just as Joseph had said to them in his interpretation.

The chief cupbearer, however, did not remember Joseph; he forgot him. Genesis 40:4-23 NIV

Poor Joseph.
Stuck in the pit.
Forgotten by men.
But not by God.

After two years had gone by (yeah, a long time) the Pharaoh had two dreams. He had no understanding of their meaning and began to feel troubled. He called everyone he could find that might be able to interpret his dreams but no one could help him.

Then, yes then, the chief cupbearer got wind of this and told Pharaoh about Joseph and what he had done while they were in prison together.

So he sent for Joseph and he was quickly brought out of the pit and into the presence of the Pharaoh.

> **Pharaoh:** *"I had a dream, and no one can interpret it. But I have heard it said of you that when you hear a dream you can interpret it."*
>
> **Joseph:** *"I cannot do it, but God will give Pharaoh the answer he desires."*
>
> **Pharaoh:** *"In my dream I was standing on the bank of the Nile, when out of the river there came up seven cows, fat and sleek, and they grazed among the reeds. After them, seven other cows came up—scrawny and very ugly and lean. I had never seen such ugly cows in all the land of Egypt. The lean, ugly cows ate up the seven fat cows that*

came up first. But even after they ate them, no one could tell that they had done so; they looked just as ugly as before. Then I woke up.

In my [second] dream I saw seven heads of grain, full and good, growing on a single stalk. After them, seven other heads sprouted—withered and thin and scorched by the east wind. The thin heads of grain swallowed up the seven good heads. I told this to the magicians, but none of them could explain it to me."

Joseph: *"The dreams of Pharaoh are one and the same. God has revealed to Pharaoh what he is about to do. The seven good cows are seven years, and the seven good heads of grain are seven years; it is one and the same dream. The seven lean, ugly cows that came up afterward are seven years, and so are the seven worthless heads of grain scorched by the east wind: They are seven years of famine.*

It is just as I said to Pharaoh: God has shown Pharaoh what he is about to do. Seven years of great abundance are coming throughout the land of Egypt, but seven years of famine will follow them. Then all the abundance in Egypt will be forgotten, and the famine will ravage the land. The abundance in the land will not be remembered, because the famine that follows it will be so severe. The reason the dream was given to Pharaoh in two forms is that the matter has been firmly decided by God, and God will do it soon.

And now let Pharaoh look for a discerning and wise man and put him in charge of the land of Egypt. Let Pharaoh appoint commissioners over the land to take a fifth of the harvest of Egypt during the seven years of abundance. They should collect all the food of these good years that are coming and store up the grain under the authority of Pharaoh, to be kept in the cities for food. This food should be held in reserve for the country, to be used during the seven years of famine that will come upon Egypt, so that the country may not be ruined by the famine." Genesis 41:17-36 NIV

Pharaoh loved the plan and so did all of his officials. Now, the only problem was finding the man to take charge of this large task. So Pharaoh asked his people if there was anyone else aside from Joseph that should take on this job. The job fell right into Joseph's lap. Everyone agreed since God made the dreams known to Joseph . . . he should also be the one to carry out the duty.

GOVERNOR

But that wasn't all. Pharaoh placed Joseph in charge of his palace and all of his people. He even stated that the only power that he held over Joseph was the throne.

Pharaoh put his signet ring on Joseph's finger, robe on his back and a gold chain around his neck. From pit to Governor, God had given Joseph power in this foreign land.

Pharaoh wouldn't let a thing be done in Egypt if Joseph's word did not affirm it. Not only did Joseph acquire clothing and power but he also was gifted a wife. He had stayed faithful and pure throughout this entire story and now his very own family line would continue. All of this by thirty years old.

So, Joseph did his job. Throughout the seven years of abundance, the land produced plenty of food. Joseph collected the food and stored it in the cities. God provided so much grain that they couldn't even keep count anymore.

The scriptures compare the grain to sand on the seashore because there was so much of it. Interestingly, next we learn that Joseph and his wife bore two sons: Manasseh ("It is because God has made me forget all my trouble and all my father's household"), and Ephraim ("It is because God has made me fruitful in the land of my suffering"). It is as if the scriptures are exclaiming God's faithfulness just as the promise of blessing that Abraham, Isaac and Jacob had received. Joseph was not the firstborn son of Jacob, but he received special attention in honor of his beloved mother Rachel.

After the seven years of abundance came seven years of famine in the land. The famine was everywhere, but the entire land of Egypt had plenty of food. When Egypt finally began to experience the famine, Pharaoh pointed the people to Joseph. He opened up storehouses in all of the cities and he began to sell food. It wasn't very long until the entire world began trekking to Egypt for food because the famine was so severe.

FAMILY

Looking at the world map, Israel and Egypt are only several hundred miles apart. Taking this into account, people had to travel a long way to aid their hunger. No cars. No modern transportation.

Can you imagine leaving home in a famine to purchase food just to survive? Sometimes I get upset because I *have to* leave my bed to get another bowl of ice cream. These people were loading up whatever food they might or might not have had in order to take a trek that they might or might not survive to provide food for their families.

> When Jacob learned that there was grain in Egypt, he said to his sons, "Why do you just keep looking at each other?" He continued, "I have heard that there is grain in Egypt. Go down there and buy some for us, so that we may live and not die."
>
> Then ten of Joseph's brothers went down to buy grain from Egypt. But Jacob did not send Benjamin, Joseph's brother, with the others, because he was afraid that harm might come to him. Genesis 42:1-4 NIV

(Did you catch that? Jacob lost his favorite son from his favorite wife. He couldn't risk losing the *other* favorite son.)

Joseph, being the governor of the land, was the one that his brothers met to purchase food. They bowed down before him with their faces to the ground.

Was this the fulfillment of the dream Joseph had back at his father's home? Did his brothers recognize him? Did they know that this was their long lost brother that they had betrayed and sold? What was the situation like?

> As soon as Joseph saw his brothers, he recognized them, but he pretended to be a stranger and spoke harshly to them.
>
> **Joseph:** "Where do you come from?"
>
> **Brothers:** "From the land of Canaan to buy food."

Although Joseph recognized his brothers, they did not recognize him. Then he remembered his dreams about them.

Joseph: "You are spies! You have come to see where our land is unprotected."

Brothers: "No, my lord, your servants have come to buy food. We are all the sons of one man. Your servants are honest men, not spies."

Joseph: "No! You have come to see where our land is unprotected."

Brothers: "Your servants were twelve brothers, the sons of one man, who lives in the land of Canaan. The youngest is now with our father, and one is no more."

Joseph: "It is just as I told you: You are spies! And this is how you will be tested: As surely as Pharaoh lives, you will not leave this place unless your youngest brother comes here. Send one of your number to get your brother; the rest of you will be kept in prison, so that your words may be tested to see if you are telling the truth. If you are not, then as surely as Pharaoh lives, you are spies!"

And Joseph put them all in custody for three days.

Joseph: "Do this and you will live, for I fear God: If you are honest men, let one of your brothers stay here in prison, while the rest of you go and take grain back for your starving households. But you must bring your youngest brother to me, so that your words may be verified and that you may not die."

Brothers (to themselves): "Surely we are being punished because of our brother. We saw how distressed he was when he pleaded with us for his life,

> *but we would not listen; that's why this distress has come on us."*
>
> **Reuben:** *"Didn't I tell you not to sin against the boy? But you wouldn't listen! Now we must give an accounting for his blood."*
>
> *They did not realize that Joseph could understand them, since he was using an interpreter. He turned away from them and began to weep, but then came back and spoke to them again. He had Simeon taken from them and bound before their eyes.*
>
> *Joseph gave orders to fill their bags with grain, to put each man's silver back in his sack, and to give them provisions for their journey. After this was done for them, they loaded their grain on their donkeys and left.*
>
> *At the place where they stopped for the night one of them opened his sack to get feed for his donkey, and he saw his silver in the mouth of his sack. "My silver has been returned," he said to his brothers. "Here it is in my sack."*

What a nice brother. He didn't even make them pay for their food.

> *Their hearts sank and they turned to each other trembling and said, "What is this that God has done to us?" Genesis 42:7-28 NIV*

So they picked up their things and departed for their long journey home. When they arrived they met their father and told him about everything that happened in Egypt.

Father, they want us to bring Benjamin back with us!

Of course Jacob does what you'd expect him to do. He's a father. His wife and son were taken from him. Simeon was taken from them in Egypt. Now his other favorite son might be in danger? Of course not! There's no way he's going! We can almost hear it for ourselves.

But after a while with little food, your stomach starts to do the thinking for you. The food the brothers had bought in Egypt was coming to an end and Jacob ordered them to go back and buy some more food.

> *Judah:* "The man warned us solemnly, 'You will not see my face again unless your brother is with you.' If you will send our brother along with us, we will go down and buy food for you. But if you will not send him, we will not go down, because the man said to us, 'You will not see my face again unless your brother is with you.'"
>
> *Jacob:* "Why did you bring this trouble on me by telling the man you had another brother?"
>
> *Brothers:* "The man questioned us closely about ourselves and our family. 'Is your father still living?' 'Do you have another brother?' We simply answered his questions. How were we to know he would say, 'Bring your brother down here'?"
>
> *Judah:* "Send the boy along with me and we will go at once, so that we and you and our children may live and not die. I myself will guarantee his safety; you can hold me personally responsible for him. If I do not bring him back to you and set him here before you, I will bear the blame before you all my life. As it is, if we had not delayed, we could have gone and returned twice." Genesis 43:3-10 NIV

Jacob finally agreed. He sent the brothers off with gifts for the man (AKA Joseph), their brother Benjamin and double the amount of silver to pay for food and reimburse him for the previous stock of food.

They hurried down to Egypt and arrived at Joseph's door. Joseph beamed with excitement and invited the brothers to his house for a party. Slaughter an animal! Prepare a meal for these men! We are going to feast!

The brothers asked each other, what are we going to do? Surely they know about the silver that was put back into our sacks! They're going to overpower us and make us slaves!

So when they arrived at Joseph's house, they met his steward and told him about the silver and offered to repay them the price and even to buy more food. But the steward calmed them down and told them everything was fine.

> "Don't be afraid. Your God, the God of your father, has given you treasure in your sacks; I received your silver." Then he brought Simeon out to them.
> Genesis 43:23 NIV

The brothers' greatest fear was to be treated as slaves, but the steward took them inside Joseph's house and provided water for them to wash their feet and food for their donkeys. They were instead treated like royalty. But they were still not aware of who Joseph was. So they prepared their gifts for his arrival.

When Joseph came home they bowed before him and presented him with gifts. Joseph saw the gifts, but he truly only cared about reuniting with family. He began to ask them about their father's health.

> **Brothers:** *"Your servant our father is still alive and well."*
>
> *And the brothers bowed down, prostrating themselves before him. Then Joseph looked about and saw his brother Benjamin, his own mother's son.*
>
> **Joseph:** *"Is this your youngest brother, the one you told me about? God be gracious to you, my son."*
>
> *Deeply moved at the sight of his brother, Joseph hurried out and looked for a place to weep. He went into his private room and wept there. After he had washed his face, he came out and, controlling himself, said,*
>
> **Joseph:** *"Serve the food."* Genesis 43:28-31 NIV

When the brother's food was served, they all looked at Benjamin because his plate had five times as much food as everyone else's.

As they were finishing eating, Joseph commanded his steward to place as much food as could be carried in each brothers sack, as well as the silver they paid with. Lastly, Joseph told him to place his very own silver cup in Benjamin's sack.

That next morning the brothers took off to head back to Canaan. Soon after they left, Joseph commanded his steward to go after them, and ask why they would steal! The brothers knew nothing of anything being stolen so they dropped their sacks and let everything be searched. The steward said if the stolen goods were to be found, then they would make the thief their slave. He searched from the oldest to the youngest and found the silver cup in Benjamin's bag. They tore their clothes in sorrow and returned back to the city with Joseph's steward (that would have been one drafty ride back).

When they arrived, Joseph asked them how they could do such a thing?

> *"What can we say to my lord?" Judah replied. "What can we say? How can we prove our innocence? God has uncovered your servants' guilt. We are now my lord's slaves—we ourselves and the one who was found to have the cup." Genesis 44:16 NIV*

But Joseph wouldn't allow all the brothers to become slaves, he only demanded the one who stole the cup to stay with him.

But our father said if we lose Benjamin, he'll die! His older brother died and this is the only son left of his wife Rachel! We cannot go back to our father if Benjamin is not with us.

Now after this long charade Joseph couldn't hold his composure any longer. *Everyone leave my presence except for these brothers!* Joseph wept so loudly that the Egyptians and Pharaoh's household heard about it.

> **Joseph:** *"I am Joseph! Is my father still living?"*
>
> *But his brothers were not able to answer him, because they were terrified at his presence.*
>
> **Joseph:** *"Come close to me. I am your brother Joseph, the one you sold into Egypt! And now, do*

not be distressed and do not be angry with yourselves for selling me here, because it was to save lives that God sent me ahead of you. For two years now there has been famine in the land, and for the next five years there will be no plowing and reaping. But God sent me ahead of you to preserve for you a remnant on earth and to save your lives by a great deliverance. So then, it was not you who sent me here, but God. He made me father to Pharaoh, lord of his entire household and ruler of all Egypt.

Now hurry back to my father and say to him, 'This is what your son Joseph says: God has made me lord of all Egypt. Come down to me; don't delay. You shall live in the region of Goshen and be near me—you, your children and grandchildren, your flocks and herds, and all you have. I will provide for you there, because five years of famine are still to come. Otherwise you and your household and all who belong to you will become destitute.'

You can see for yourselves, and so can my brother Benjamin, that it is really I who am speaking to you. Tell my father about all the honor accorded me in Egypt and about everything you have seen. And bring my father down here quickly." Genesis 45:3-13 NIV

Then Joseph hugged his brother Benjamin as he wept and kissed all of his brothers and celebrated their reunion.

Soon, news reached Pharaoh and all his officials and they were happy for him. *Tell your brothers to get your father, your family and all of their animals and move here! Settle your family in Goshen; it's the best land of Egypt! They will live here and enjoy great foods! Go take carts to help them travel back here to their new home. I will also give them new clothes, large sums of food and money. Now hurry!*

So the brothers took off and headed to their father's house in Canaan (yes, the Land of Promise. The Gift! I felt like it had been too long since I last said that). Once they arrived, they told their father all that had happened! Joseph is alive! Not only is he alive – he's the ruler of all Egypt! But Jacob could not believe what he was hearing. So the brothers showed him the carts and all that they'd brought back and Jacob believed! Jacob said,

> *"I'm convinced! My son Joseph is still alive. I will go and see him before I die.'" Genesis 45:28 NIV*

So they left. All sixty-six of them! They took everything and headed down to Egypt. On the way Jacob offered sacrifices to God at a place called Beersheba. That night God spoke to him and said,

> *"I am God, the God of your father," he said. "Do not be afraid to go down to Egypt, for I will make you into a great nation there. I will go down to Egypt with you, and I will surely bring you back again. And Joseph's own hand will close your eyes." Genesis 46:3-4 NIV*

When they were close, Jacob sent Judah ahead to ask Joseph for directions to Goshen (you know, because an army of sixty-six people wouldn't be that difficult to walk right up to the palace and ask).

Once the family arrived at the spot they would call home, Joseph arrived and threw his arms around his father for the first time in years. Oh, the tears.

BLESSINGS

Sometime later, Joseph was told his father was getting very ill. Joseph grabbed his two sons, Manasseh and Ephraim, and took off to see Jacob. He was so ill that it took all that was within him just to sit up.

> *Jacob:* "I never expected to see your face again, and now God has allowed me to see your children too."

Then Joseph brought his sons before his father strategically placing Manasseh on Jacob's right side and Ephraim on his left. But Jacob switched his hands.

> *Jacob:* "May the God before whom my fathers Abraham and Isaac walked faithfully, the God who has been my shepherd
>
> all my life to this day, the Angel who has delivered me from all harm—may he bless these boys. May they be called by my name and the names of my fathers Abraham and Isaac, and may they increase greatly on the earth."
>
> When Joseph saw his father placing his right hand on Ephraim's head he was displeased; so he took hold of his father's hand to move it from Ephraim's head to Manasseh's head.
>
> *Joseph:* "No, my father, this one is the firstborn; put your right hand on his head."
>
> *Jacob:* "I know, my son, I know. He too will become a people, and he too will become great. Nevertheless, his younger brother will be greater than he, and his descendants will become a group of nations. I am about to die, but God will be with you

and take you back to the land of your fathers."
Genesis 48:11-21 NIV

After this private blessing Jacob called the rest of his sons to his side to give final blessings.

"Reuben, you are my firstborn. You are strong and honorable but you have sinned against me as an adulterer. For this you will not receive my blessing.

Simeon and Levi, you are violent in anger (remember Shechem?). Your people will be scattered in Israel.

Judah, your brothers will praise you. The scepter will not depart from you until he to whom it belongs shall come.

Zebulan will live by the sea and be a haven for ships.

Issachar is strong. He saw that the land was good and restful.

Dan shall judge his people as one of the tribes of Israel.

Raiders will raid Gad but he will raid their heels.

Asher shall be rich.

Naphtali is a doe let loose. He gives beautiful words.

Joseph is fruitful. He was attacked but stood strong. May God continue to bless you with heavenly blessings.

Benjamin is a ravenous wolf. In the morning he devours the prey and in the evening he divides the spoil."

When the blessings were over, he gave special orders for where he wanted to be buried and took his last breath.

After the embalming was finished and the mourning period was over, Joseph went to Pharaoh and asked if he could take his father's body and bury it in the land of Canaan beside Abraham and Isaac. Pharaoh agreed, then the caravan of family, Pharaoh's servants and elders of Egypt departed for Canaan for the funeral.

Now that Jacob was buried, the brothers feared, *what if Joseph has held a grudge against us for all the wrong we did to him?* So they sent a message to Joseph stating that their father before his death charged Joseph to forgive them for their wrongdoing.

> *But Joseph said to them, "Do not be afraid, for am I in God's place? As for you, you meant evil against me, but God meant it for good in order to bring about this present result, to preserve many people alive. So therefore, do not be afraid; I will provide for you and your little ones." So he comforted them and spoke kindly to them. Genesis 50:19-21 NIV*

Joseph was able to live a full life and watch his son's families grow in his old age. When his death was near, he gathered his brothers and gave them his blessing: *God will take care of you and our family. He will bring you out of the land of Egypt and back into the land of Abraham, Isaac and Jacob.*

Now, let's talk about the baby who delivered a nation.

MOSES

CHAPTER SEVEN

Take off your sandals, for the place where you are standing is holy ground. Exodus 3:5 NIV

THE EARLY YEARS

And that sets the stage for the second book of the Bible, Exodus. There are just some words that you read, pass over, and don't really think much more about them. Take Platypus for example. The Greek word Platus means flat and Pous means foot. So, flatfoot. Platypus just sounds a lot more fun to say!

But then take the word Exodus. It means exit. No break down to the word. No double meaning. Just exit. While in college I had the chance to study abroad in Greece. When I first arrived and looked for an exit sign at the airport I saw EXODUS. This was the first time I realized what the word actually meant. And it is what it says it is. It's a book about leaving.

After Joseph, his brothers and all their generation had died a new king came to power that didn't know Joseph. The Israelites were strong, fruitful, and large in number and Egypt's new king didn't like any bit of it.

> *"Look," he said to his people, "the Israelites have become far too numerous for us. Come, we must deal shrewdly with them or they will become even more numerous and, if war breaks out, will join our enemies, fight against us and leave the country."*
> *Exodus 1:9-10 NIV*

To prohibit this, Egypt made Joseph's descendants slaves. They were oppressed. They were forced to build store cities, Ramses and Pithom, to store excess food. Joseph, while alive and in command of Egypt, built store cities to help aid the nation in time of famine. But this new Pharaoh was using them to take advantage of his people. He was making the people poorer and himself wealthier. Egypt had quickly become a land of injustice and inequality.

(Side Note: Ramses was the city that Joseph and his Pharaoh gave the Israelite's to settled in at the end of Genesis.)

The Israelites were worked like dogs. Their lives were made bitter with harsh labor. The more they were oppressed the more the nation of Israel grew. The king became angry and told the Israelite midwives to kill any boys but to let the girls live; thus the nation wouldn't strengthen and turn on Egypt. But the midwives feared God more than the king and didn't obey his command. This pleased God and he multiplied the nation even more. But this did not please Pharaoh so he ordered,

MOSES

> *"Every Hebrew boy that is born you must throw into the Nile, but let every girl live."* Exodus 1:22 NIV

Against Pharaoh's order, the nation of Israel continued to grow and one of Levi's descendants gave birth to a son. *You know the rule. You know the current way of life. The boy couldn't live.* But instead of killing the boy, the mother hid him for several months. After the hiding became too difficult, she put him in a basket and let him drift down the Nile thinking maybe an Egyptian could care for him. The baby's sister watched from afar as he floated down the river right near Pharaoh's palace.

Just then, Pharaoh's daughter, Bithiah, had gone out to bathe and saw the basket. She opened it and noticed he was a Hebrew. At an opportune time, his sister walked up to the woman and asked:

> *"Shall I go and get one of the Hebrew women to nurse the baby for you?"*
>
> *"Yes, go," she answered. So the girl went and got the baby's mother. Pharaoh's daughter said to her, "Take this baby and nurse him for me, and I will pay you."*
>
> *So the girl went and got the baby's mother. When the child grew older, she took him to Pharaoh's daughter and he became her son. She named him Moses, saying, "I drew him out of the water."*
> Exodus 2:7-10 NIV

Not only does Moses' mother get him back, but she is paid indirectly by Pharaoh to take care of him.

(Let me get this straight. Pharaoh ordered that all baby boys be killed, yet he is the one that pays for one of the babies to be raised. The one who soon would save the entire Israelite nation. You cannot tell me that the Bible is boring!)

Somewhere along the line Moses came to know that he was a Hebrew. He began to watch the Hebrews labor in pain as the Egyptians treated them harshly. One day he saw an Egyptian beating a Hebrew and was filled with anger. He looked around and noticed no one was watching so he killed the Egyptian for his unkindness.

The next day he saw two Hebrews fighting and walked up to the one who was in the wrong. *Why are you hitting your fellow brother?* Moses didn't anticipate his reply. *Are you thinking of killing me like you did that Egyptian?* Word got out and Pharaoh wanted him dead! Moses fled to the city of Midian. Now, if you were thinking Midian is anywhere close to Egypt you'd be wrong. Midian is in present day Saudi Arabia. So he booked it!

Once Moses arrived in Midian, he sat near a well. So would I! Most of his trek was desert. And to be honest Midian . . . well, it's a desert itself.

But he wasn't alone for long. Jethro (or shortly referred to as Reuel), the city's priest, had seven daughters and they had come to draw water for their father's flocks. As soon as they arrived, some shepherds drove off their flocks and Moses stepped in and took care of it. You see, Moses was still wearing his Egyptian attire and was treated as an Egyptian.

Jethro heard of the kind gesture Moses had done and invited him to eat with his family. Not only does he feed Moses, but also offers his daughter, Zipporah, to him in marriage! (That's a pretty nice thank you if I say so myself).

By this point, the Pharaoh that Moses knew had died and the Israelites cried out in their oppression!

> God heard their groaning and he remembered his covenant with Abraham, with Isaac and with Jacob. So God looked on the Israelites and was concerned about them. Exodus 2:24-25 NIV

THE CALL OF MOSES

One day, Moses was working tending his father-in-law's flock and arrived at Mount Horeb. Now, Mount Horeb wasn't any ordinary place. It was also called the Mountain of God (Mt. Sinai).

> There the angel of the Lord appeared to him in flames of fire from within a bush. Moses saw that though the bush was on fire it did not burn up. So Moses thought, "I will go over and see this strange sight—why the bush does not burn up."
>
> When the Lord saw that he had gone over to look, God called to him from within the bush,
>
> **God:** "Moses! Moses! Do not come any closer, take off your sandals, for the place where you are standing is holy ground. I am the God of your father, the God of Abraham, the God of Isaac and the God of Jacob."
>
> At this, Moses hid his face, because he was afraid to look at God.

> God: "I have indeed seen the misery of my people in Egypt. I have heard them crying out because of their slave drivers, and I am concerned about their suffering. So I have come down to rescue them from the hand of the Egyptians and to bring them up out of that land into a good and spacious land, a land flowing with milk and honey. And now the cry of the Israelites has reached me, and I have seen the way the Egyptians are oppressing them. So now, go! I am sending you to Pharaoh to bring my people the Israelites out of Egypt." Exodus 3:2-10 NIV

What a conversation!
Did the sky go dark when the fire went ablaze?
Was God's voice deep?
Did it sound like Morgan Freeman?
So many questions!

But Moses didn't do what we might expect.

> Moses: "Who am I that I should go to Pharaoh and bring the Israelites out of Egypt?"

> God: "I will be with you. And this will be the sign to you that it is I who have sent you: When you have brought the people out of Egypt, you will worship God on this mountain." Exodus 3:11-12 NIV

So what happened next?
Does he do it?

Moses continued to ramble on. *What if the Israelites question me? What if they ask who sent me?*

> God: "**I am who I am.** This is what you are to say to the Israelites: 'I AM has sent me to you. The Lord, the God of your fathers—the God of Abraham, the

God of Isaac and the God of Jacob—has sent me to you.'" Exodus 3:14-15 NIV

Do you feel the significance of what just happened? God, for the first time ever, had revealed his name to the world! *This is my name forever. Call me by it for all generations.*

Moses' life was changed in an instant.

Go to the elders of Israel and tell them that I have sent you to them. Let them know I have heard their cries and that I will deliver them to the land of the Canaanites, Hittites, Amorites, Perizzites, Hivites and Jebusites. The land is fruitful and flowing with milk and honey. You and the elders will meet with the Pharoah and explain that I am leading you out of Egypt. They won't like it but I will take care of that. Every woman is to ask her neighbor for silver, gold and clothing. I will provide these things for you before your journey.

Moses STILL didn't feel qualified for the job

What if they don't trust me? They may not believe me!
Here are some miracles. Do them and they'll believe you!

I'm not a very good speaker.
Who gave you your mouth? I will give you the words to say.

There's probably someone better suited for this.
I'll put your brother Aaron beside you. He will speak for you.

After some assurance from God, Moses finally agreed to follow through with the task!

After asking permission from his father-in-law to go back to Egypt (while leaving out a few details about what he was exactly going to do), God told Moses that those who wanted to kill him were now dead. So he grabbed his wife and sons and trekked back to the land of Egypt.

Then God told Moses, when you return to Egypt you are to perform the miracles I've given you power to do in front of Pharaoh. But I will harden his heart and he won't let my people go. So say to him, the Lord says Israel is His firstborn son. Let him go so he may worship me. But if you refuse to let him go; I will kill your firstborn son.

Hardening of the heart?
Was God just trying to pick a fight?
What was the motivation here?

> *The Lord said to [Moses' brother] Aaron, "Go into the wilderness to meet Moses." So he met Moses at the mountain of God and kissed him. Then Moses told Aaron everything the Lord had sent him to say, and also about all the signs he had commanded him to perform.*
>
> *Moses and Aaron brought together all the elders of the Israelites, and Aaron told them everything the Lord had said to Moses. He also performed the signs before the people, and they believed. And when they heard that the Lord was concerned about them and had seen their misery, they bowed down and worshiped. Exodus 4:27-31 NIV*

Just let that sit with you for a while.

Imagine with me.

The Egyptians had enslaved your family for years.
You've seen misery. Death. Destruction.
You've heard weeping day after day.
You cry out to God for help but don't feel heard.
It's a vicious cycle.
Then something different happened.
You're told God heard you.
You're told He's rescuing you.
You see the light when darkness surrounds you.
You fall to your knees in worship because it's all you can do.

THE MISSION

Moses and Aaron went boldly before Pharaoh. *The Lord, our God, demands our release to go worship Him! But Pharaoh shot back with who is this Lord that I should obey him? I am the only god you should be worried about!*

In other words, no.

Pharaoh was angry. He told Moses and Aaron that the Israelites needed to get back to work and ordered the slave drivers to push more work onto Israel.

The Israelites were livid. *May the Lord judge you Moses! You've made us obnoxious to the Egyptians. Thanks for nothing! We'll surely die for this.*

Now Moses was caught in the middle between God and the Israelites.

> *Moses:* "Why, Lord, why have you brought trouble on this people? Is this why you sent me? Ever since I went to Pharaoh to speak in your name, he has brought trouble on this people, and you have not rescued your people at all."
>
> *God:* "Now you will see what I will do to Pharaoh: Because of my mighty hand he will let them go; because of my mighty hand he will drive them out of his country.
>
> *I am the Lord. I appeared to Abraham, to Isaac and to Jacob as God Almighty, but by my name the Lord I did not make myself fully known to them. I also established my covenant with them to give them the land of Canaan, where they resided as foreigners. Moreover, I have heard the groaning of the Israelites, whom the Egyptians are enslaving, and I have remembered my covenant.*
>
> *Therefore, say to the Israelites: 'I am the Lord, and I will bring you out from under the yoke of the Egyptians. I will free you from being slaves to them, and I will redeem you with an outstretched arm and with mighty acts of judgment. I will take you as my own people, and I will be your God. And I will bring you to the land I swore with uplifted hand to give to Abraham, to Isaac and to Jacob. I will give it to you as a possession. I am the Lord.'"* Exodus 5:22; 6:1-8 NIV

Did you see that? The gift. God made the same promise to Moses that He made to Abraham, Isaac and Jacob. This is much bigger than being freed from slavery. The people of Israel are being called back to their home.

So Moses jumped up and ran to tell the Israelites what God had in store for them, but due to their discouragement they didn't listen. The reality of harsh labor and cruel treatment kept them from seeing the light at the end of the tunnel.

Lord, they won't listen to me! I'm trying to fulfill the task you've given me but they won't budge. We can almost feel Moses' frustration.

But God commanded Moses to demand Pharaoh to let the Israelites go. Basically, *Moses, I get that you're scared and feel unqualified. But just do what I ask of you. I'm beside you. I will speak through you, act through you, and lead you the entire way.*

So Moses took off. He went before Pharaoh demanding the release of the Israelites but is denied due to God's hardening of Pharaoh's heart. But without hardening Pharaoh's heart would he have let the Israelites go?

Next, God performed miracles and nine plagues before Pharaoh, but still Pharaoh's answer was "no" for their release. Interestingly, God didn't need to harden Pharaoh's heart until the fifth plague because Pharaoh's heart was already so corroded. The Nile River turned to blood; frogs filled the country; gnats and flies swarmed the people; their livestock died; boils plagued the Egyptians; hail devoured their land; swarms of locust ate what outlasted the hail; and darkness fell upon the land for three days. The scriptures say that you could *feel* the darkness. Yet nothing harmed the Israelites.

After all this, Pharaoh still denied Moses!

But, God had one more plague up his sleeve. He told Moses that this would be the plague that would result in their escape. *Tell the Israelites to collect articles of silver and gold from their neighbors. Trust me, I've made them regard you highly; they will do as you ask.*

Moses went boldly before Pharaoh and explained the final plague; the plague of the firstborn. God would kill the firstborn of every Egyptian and of their livestock. And to our surprise Pharaoh, even though he'd seen all the wonders God had done, still denied Moses and Aaron their release because God had hardened Pharaoh's heart.

God wanted to make his power known to the Egyptians. The Pharaoh viewed himself as a god, but God was making it known that He is the One and only God. What seems to be barbaric and cruel was setting the stage for the entire world to know the one true God. Since the fall of humanity God had been redeeming His people back to Him, and back to the way it was originally created to be—good.

THE PASSOVER

God told Moses and Aaron that what was about to happen would be so significant that it would change history. *This month will be the first month of your year. Gather the community and tell the families to each slaughter a lamb for dinner; it must be a one-year-old male without any defects,* which represent Israel's firstborn males who are young and filled with vigor. *Take the blood and mark your doorframes for in the night I will pass over (Passover) Egypt and strike down every firstborn of both people and animals. I will see the blood on your houses and spare you. You are to roast the lamb over fire with all of its body still intact. You will eat bitter herbs and unleavened bread along with the lamb.* For the bitter herbs represent the bitter work you've endured in Egypt and the unleavened bread represent the event's haste. *When you eat, your cloak is to be tucked into your belt, sandals on your feet and staff in hand.* Eat in haste. This represents an attitude of urgency and readiness for what God has in store for the Israelites. *Generations to come will remember this day and celebrate this festival of Unleavened Bread because it is on this day that I will deliver you out of Egypt.*

The Israelites did just as Moses and Aaron had said.

At midnight God passed over the land and struck down the firstborn of every Egyptian and their animals. There were loud cries heard throughout the entire land. There was not one Egyptian home without someone dead.

EXODUS: EXIT

> *Pharaoh: "Up! Leave my people, you and the Israelites! Go, worship the Lord as you have requested. Take your flocks and herds, as you have said, and go. And also bless me." Exodus 12:31-32 NIV*

So the Israelites were out of there! They carried the unleavened yeast in troughs on their shoulders. They asked their neighbors for silver, gold and clothing! God was already ahead of things and made the Egyptians favorably disposed toward the Israelites so they would give the Israelites all they needed for their travels. The Israelites were six hundred thousand fighting men plus women and children. Before they made it completely out of Egypt, they camped out for the night while God watched out for them.

During the Israelites' rest, God told Moses to consecrate to Him every firstborn male. God would use them for a holy purpose. Mainly, leading their families in accordance to God's commands. This story of deliverance was to be taught to all generations for years to come.

The time had finally come for the Israelites to officially leave the land of Egypt. Though traveling north through the land of the Philistines to the Promised Land was shorter, God directed Moses to travel across the Red Sea and through the desert. So they took the bones of their patriarch Joseph (as they promised they'd bury him near his father and grandfathers) and took off!

God led the Israelites by pillar of cloud by day and a pillar of fire by night. He never left the people in their journey.

While the Israelites were traveling, God hardened Pharaoh's heart one last time and made him aware that the Israelites had fled.

Pharaoh took his best chariots, his best men, and pursued the Israelites!

What happened next really sets the tone for the Israelites moving forward. They're following Moses but they weren't one hundred percent onboard.

The Israelites looked up and saw the Egyptians and thought, *why have you brought us out here to die? Didn't we ask you to leave us alone in Egypt? They were harsh but at least we were alive!*

But Moses comforted the people. *God is on our side. Do not be afraid. The Egyptians you see today you will never see again. God is fighting for you.*

Then God said to Moses, *stretch out your arm with staff in hand and I will part the Red Sea for you to go through it.*

The pillar of cloud and pillar of fire then moved from in front to behind the Israelites—between them and the Egyptians. While the Egyptians chased after the Israelites, God jammed their chariots and made it difficult to catch them.

Once the Israelites crossed the sea to the other side, God required Moses to stretch out his arms again to close the sea upon the Egyptians who had been chasing after them. The water flowed back just as it was before and swept the Egyptians up.

When the Israelites saw the Egyptians dead on the shore, they saw the mighty hand of God and put their trust in God and in Moses as His servant.

If you're reading this story for the first time, isn't this gruesome? If you've heard this story a thousand times, let this story be what it is. People died. Real lives were lost. But this story couldn't have happened any other way. If the Egyptians hadn't died, they would've continued to pursue the Israelites. If the Israelites had stayed in Egypt, they would've never truly been their own people. They would've been influenced by the Egyptian culture and not truly be a people of God. God needed them to be set apart.

In this time of death, destruction and deliverance the Israelites began to worship God. They started singing, "The Lord is my strength and my defense! He has become my salvation. He is my God, and I will praise Him. The Lord is a warrior; the Lord is His name."

Their previous fright and ill-confidence in God and Moses had all shied away. In front of them was a journey through the desert and a leap of faith. All they had ever known was in Egypt. Would they keep their faith and stick together, or fall apart?

SHAPING A NATION: GODS AT WAR

CHAPTER EIGHT

You yourselves have seen what I did to Egypt, and how I carried you on eagles' wings and brought you to myself. Now if you obey me fully and keep my covenant, then out of all nations you will be my treasured possession.
Exodus 19:4-5 NIV

TRAVEL TIME

The whole Israelite community set out and came to the Desert of Sin near Mt Sinai . . . the second month after they had come out of Egypt. In the desert the whole community grumbled against Moses and Aaron: "If only we had died by the Lord's hand in Egypt! There we sat around pots of meat and ate all the food we wanted, but you have brought us out into this desert to starve us!

Two months into their journey and they had little faith in God yet again.

> Then the Lord said to Moses, "I will rain down bread from heaven for you. The people are to go out each day and gather enough for that day. In this way I will test them and see whether they will follow my instructions. On the sixth day they are to prepare what they bring in, and that is to be twice as much as they gather on the other days." Exodus 16:1-5 NIV

God watches over his flock. Can't you sense the fatherly love that God has for the Israelites? God led them, fed them and protected them. But, when there was a need and God hadn't stepped in right when they wanted Him to, they were upset.

Do you notice what God was doing? He was testing and equipping His people to follow Him. For several hundred years the Israelites have been lost. They'd watched the Egyptians and probably took part in their customs. Before Joseph brought his family to Egypt, they were a specific people with their own customs and they followed God. Now they had no true identity. God was trying to build up their character to be a people of God.

God tested His people by giving them simple commands. He told the people to gather enough food for their day on days one through five. Those who listened to God's command were full and fed. Those who didn't listen to God, and kept food until morning woke up to maggot-infested smelly food. God was teaching His people to follow Him.

God wanted Israel to be an example to the people around them. If God's people were acting out, why would anyone else listen to Him?

On the sixth day the people were to gather twice as much because the seventh day was Sabbath, a day of rest. On that day no food would be provided except for what they stored up on the previous day.

God told the Israelites to keep some of the manna He provided to show generations to come the food that He provided them with in the desert. So they did as He required and stored them in jars. They ate manna for forty years until they came to the Promised Land. Forty years!

As the people traveled from the Desert of Sin, the people became thirsty and there was no water to drink. So the people did as people do when they get upset. They yelled and cried and demanded water from Moses.

Moses got angry. Of course he did! *Why put God to the test?*

And the people got even angrier. *Why did you bring us out here to die?* As if they didn't have a better phrase to cry.

So God *creatively* made Moses strike a rock with his staff and water began pouring out. He could've given water any other way, but I think God was saying . . . *even out of a rock I can provide water for you. Just trust me, okay?*

PROTECT AND CONQUER. As if Moses wasn't already having enough trouble, a group of Amalekites came and attacked the Israelites.

(Side Note: Amalekites were the descendants of Jacob's twin brother Esau. Jacob was later renamed Israel. So, this battle was one between Israel and Esau. The brotherly quarrel was still far from over.)

Moses grabbed his sidekick Joshua and told him to quickly gather an army. Joshua grabbed some men and began to fight back while Moses stood on top of a hill with his staff in hand. When his staff was raised the Israelites were winning, but whenever his arms grew weak and the staff was lowered the Amalekites were winning. So you better believe they kept Moses' arms remained raised so the battle would be won in Israel's favor.

This was another situation of God showing His people that He was on their side. He was their protector and deliverer.

It can be easy for us on this side of things to say, *how could they have not just trusted in God? He was there, present right in front of them*. But the truth is, God in all of recorded history has only shown himself physically to a small number of people. Most of the Israelites knew God similar to how we know him now. We have faith that He is here. We feel His power. But Moses was the one hearing God directly. Everyone else heard from Moses.

So, let's be patient with the Israelites. We continually do what the Israelites were doing. There is no issue when things go well for us! But when things aren't going so well, we question if He is there. And if He is, is He on our side?

By this point the people truly needed not only a person to guide them to the Promised Land but also some sort of government. So Moses made himself judge over the people of Israel. But Moses' father-in-law, Jethro, met him near Sinai and brought Moses' wife and sons along with him. In their reunion, Jethro praised God for all of the good He was doing with the people of Israel.

When Jethro heard that Moses made himself judge over Israel, he urged Moses to place more judges in position. So it was then that Israel was divided not only into tribes but each tribe had their own set of officials to help Moses govern the people and keep peace within the nation.

THE LAW AT MT SINAI

Three months after the people left Egypt they arrived at the base of Mount Sinai.

> *Then Moses went up to God, and the Lord called to him from the mountain and said, "This is what you are to say to the people of Israel: 'You yourselves have seen what I did to Egypt, and how I carried you on eagles' wings and brought you to myself. Now if you obey me fully and keep my covenant, then out of all nations you will be my treasured possession. Although the whole earth is mine, you will be for me a kingdom of priests and a holy nation.' These are the words you are to speak to the Israelites." Exodus 19:3-6 NIV*

I love this. We often get mixed up in Israel versus the world as if God only cared about Israel. But this is not the case. Israel was being groomed to be *the* example for the rest of the earth to take after.

Put limits around the base of the mountain. No person or animal may touch the mountain or pass the limits or they must be put to death. I will descend in smoke and fire around the mountain. Bring the people to me so that they may see me speaking to you. God, for the first time ever, made Himself physically known to the Israelites. This was another situation for God to make His strength known to His people. Then God told Moses to climb the mountain alone to speak to Him there.

Have you ever climbed a mountain? Now, I don't know how tall this mountain is, but I do know it's extremely tiring to climb. Once Moses got to the top of the mountain God directed him to climb back down and bring back his brother Aaron. So Moses did as God commanded. Phew!

When Moses returned God had a lot to say to him.

> *"I am the Lord your God, who brought you out of Egypt, out of the land of slavery. You shall have no other gods before me."*
>
> *"You shall not make for yourself an image in the form of anything in heaven above or on the earth beneath. For I, the Lord your God, am a jealous God"*
>
> *"You shall not misuse the name of the Lord your God."*
>
> *"Remember the Sabbath day by keeping it holy."*
>
> *"Honor your father and your mother"*
>
> *"You shall not murder."*
>
> *"You shall not commit adultery."*
>
> *"You shall not steal."*
>
> *"You shall not give false testimony against your neighbor."*

SHAPING A NATION: GODS AT WAR

"You shall not covet." Exodus 20:2-5, 7-8, 12-17 NIV

When God said these things, the people saw smoke, lightning and thunder and trembled in fear. They cried out to Moses, *tell us what God has said but do not have God speak to us for we'll die.*

Moses calmed the people and explained that fearing God is a good thing. It keeps us from sinning. Then Moses returned to the thick cloud where God was.

When Moses returned to God, He had plenty more to say. He gave laws against worshiping idols and commanded them to build an altar to offer sacrifices to Him. There were laws about treating people with respect and dignity. Laws about keeping the Sabbath holy. He even gave a command to celebrate with Him three times a year through festivals. Check out Exodus chapters 20 through 23.

After saying these things God encouraged Moses, *I am sending an angel ahead of you. Listen to him and don't rebel against him. I will drive out the peoples who currently live in the land I am gifting you. I will defeat these people and you will live in their land. Crush the idols in the land so that you won't be tempted to worship their gods. Only worship the Lord your God. Do not let any of these people live in your land for they will cause you to sin against Me.*

The Israelites agreed to all that God had commanded of them. Moses got up early the next day and built an altar to the Lord where he placed twelve stone pillars, one for each tribe, to make offerings to God in obedience to His commandments.

Then Moses, Joshua, Aaron's sons, along with the seventy elders of Israel, went back up the mountain. But Moses and Joshua went up a little further to where God was. God wrote down the law and commandments on stone tablets and gave them to Moses for the Israelites.

For forty days and forty nights Moses stayed on the mountain with God while He continued to coach him to lead the nation. This wasn't seminary; this was a one on one intensive course with God on leadership.

During those forty days God explained to Moses how to build a tabernacle (AKA the first temple) and how to perform offerings within it. Moses was given blueprints for the Ark of the Covenant which would hold the Ten Commandments, among other things. God explained exactly what furniture and accessories He wanted to be within the tabernacle; including a room called The Most Holy Place where God's Spirit would reside. The High Priest was the only person who could go in this place and they had to be from the tribe of Levi. There were laws about the courtyards of the tabernacle and even what clothes the priests could wear.

God then called Moses to ordain Aaron and his sons as Levitical priests. It took seven days to carry out the ordination according to God's requirements. God then gave laws of priestly duty for Aaron and his sons to carry out.

God hadn't missed a step in fulfilling His great plan to redeem humanity back to holiness.

THAT GOLDEN CALF. When God was finished with him, Moses went down the mountain to see that the Israelites had already turned to looking for another god in his absence. In their waiting, they began to doubt that he was ever going to return.

God has surely forgotten us! Let's make gods who will now take care of us!

The people created a golden calf and worshiped it. But Aaron's conscience felt compromised. So he built an altar in front of it to the Lord and the people made sacrifices to both God and the calf.

Moses was angry
God was livid.

I have fed, clothed, protected and delivered these people yet they were so quick to turn from what I've commanded of them! I'm going to kill them! Literally, I'm going to start over with Moses and make a great nation.

Moses burned red with anger. He threw down the stone tablets that God had given him and they crumbled into pieces. He melted the calf into liquid and ground the tablets into powder and made the Israelites drink it.

Moses took it a little further than soap in the mouth.

Then Moses shouted, *if you are for the Lord come to me!* So many of the Levites ran to him. Moses commanded each man to strap a sword to their side and to go back and forth through camp killing those who did not obey the Lord.

Dreadful.
Violent.
Purging.
Cleansing of the community.

Moses returned to the Lord and pleaded forgiveness on the Israelites' behalf. God responded with the promise that He'd made to Abraham, Isaac and Jacob. *Leave this place and lead these people to the land of promise. It is a land flowing with milk and honey. But I will not join you on your journey because you are a stiff-necked people and I might destroy you.*

God loves His people so much, but it pains Him to watch them fall away from Him. He loved them enough to let them live (those who were left that is) but He needed a little distance for the time being.

In hearing this, the people began to mourn. They understood, to a degree, what they had done to God. I know how I feel when I make a mistake, but to hear how God felt about it would be rough.

THE FACE OF GOD. Now it was custom for Moses to take a tent and pitch it outside of the camp where He would talk to God. When Moses went in to the tent, the people would rise in front of their tents. As Moses went into the tent, the pillar of cloud would come down at the entrance of Moses' tent while God spoke with Moses. Whenever the people saw the cloud at the tent, they would worship in front of their tents.

Moses inquired the Lord about who would lead the people to the Promised Land. *This nation is your people. If your presence does not go with us, we will not leave this place. How else will the people know you are pleased with us? What will separate us from the other nations?*

And the Lord said to Moses, *I am pleased with you so I will send my presence ahead of you to lead you.*

Then Moses asked God to show His glory.

But God told Moses, *you have my goodness, mercy and compassion, but I cannot let you see my face, for no one may see me and live.*

Next, God placed Moses at a cleft in a rock nearby and He said, *I will cover you with my hand as I pass by you. Then I will remove my hand and you'll see my back but my face will not be seen.*

TABLETS ROUND TWO. The Lord said to Moses, "Chisel out two stone tablets like the first ones, and I will write on them the words that were on the first tablets, which you broke. Be ready in the morning, and then come up on Mount Sinai. Present yourself to me there on top of the mountain. No one is to come with you or be seen anywhere on the mountain; not even the flocks and herds." Exodus 34:1-3 NIV

So Moses chiseled out the two stone tablets similar to the first ones and went back up the mountain to meet God there.

As God arrived, He declared His faithfulness and righteousness before Moses. Basically, *I love you. Though you all royally screwed up, I am choosing to still lead you to the land I've promised your ancestors. I'm not letting you destroy My plan.*

You know, the gift.

But God doesn't do this without restating His expectations that He has for this nation. *Remember my commandments! Remember my laws. These are good for you to live by.*

When Moses came back down to the people, his face shined so bright that everyone was afraid. Moses was literally wearing his emotions on his face. His time speaking to the Lord was so precious and impactful that his face glowed.

Moses called the people near and gave them God's commands. After the conversation, Moses put a veil over his face and he wore it unless he went to speak to the Lord. Only then would he remove his veil.

CONSTRUCTION

Moses then put skilled workers in charge of constructing the Tabernacle. Everyone was called to bring together all the materials needed to construct the Tabernacle, Ark of Covenant, Lamp Stand, Table, Courtyard, Priest's clothing, etc. There were people making curtains, sculpting wood and forging metal. Everyone had a job. God's temple was finally going to be made.

At this time in history different nations had their own gods and they "resided" in temples. But our God is different. He is the God above all Gods. His temple had certain specifications and every piece of it had significant meaning.

Once construction had finished the Israelites showed Moses all they had done. God had such specific directions for every item and Moses needed to inspect everything to be sure that it met God's standards.

Once Moses' inspection was over, he saw that they had done everything just as the Lord had commanded. So he blessed them.

> *Then the cloud covered the tent of meeting, and the glory of the Lord filled the tabernacle. Moses could not enter the tent of meeting because the cloud had settled on it, and the glory of the Lord filled the tabernacle. Exodus 40:34-35 NIV*

Throughout the Israelites slavery they cried out for God and didn't hear Him. The book of Exodus ends with God being present with His people. He was making sure that they knew He was different from the Egyptian gods. He is the God that comes down. He is the God that is among us.

LEVITICUS

Exodus ends and Leviticus begins with Moses standing outside of the Tabernacle while God spoke to him from within.

The Tabernacle was also called the Tent of Meeting and sat in the middle of camp. It was the place where God and humanity met. Other nations had tents similar to this where they would bring food and offerings to appease their gods. But those gods never responded. But *this* God was present. *This* God spoke to His people. This God didn't look like the world around them and He didn't want His people to look like the world either.

The breadth of this book covers laws that God wanted Moses to preserve and lead the people to obey. These weren't suggestions for the people; they were orders. These laws covered Burnt Offerings, Grain Offerings, Fellowship Offerings, Sin Offerings, Guilt Offerings, laws about clean and unclean foods, childbirth, diseases, holiness, festival observances, blessings and curses, and laws pertaining to things set apart for God.

God is holy and needed His people to be holy. Do you remember what happened in Genesis 3? The Fall of humanity, right? Since the fall, God had been working to redeem the world back to a lifestyle of holiness; the way it was originally intended to be. It was through the Israelites that God chose to redeem the world and they needed to look the part.

In looking through history, we notice that people don't change very much in their thinking. If you are a farmer, you realize that you need sunshine and rain for your crops to grow properly. If they don't, you would assume that the crops got too much sun or not enough. You might consider that you didn't get enough rain during that season. After a while, you might assume that there is something that controls the sun and the rain. You might even begin praying to the sun. After a while they become gods on which you are dependent.

Then you might get curious if you did something to anger the gods when things didn't go your way. Next, you might offer a gift to these gods. But the difficulty grew because you couldn't hear from these gods. They didn't speak.

But this God was different.

God gave order to the Israelites. While other nations were running in circles trying to appease their gods, this God was making an effort to be present with His people.

God took the people where they were and spun everything on its head. *The Egyptians made offerings to appease gods who aren't real. But you, when you sin against me or your neighbor, you will make an offering to me and I will hear your plea.*

There were five types of offerings that people could bring before God. The Burnt Offering was an offering for purification between man and God. All offerings are Burnt Offerings. The Grain Offering was the only offering that did not require the shedding of blood. A person would find the finest of grain (and you can imagine being in the desert it was troublesome finding grain) and burn it as an aroma for the Lord. The Fellowship Offering was an offering that took place in one of three occasions: Giving thanks to God for an unforeseen blessing, a time of dire need or alongside a fulfilled vow. The Guilt Offering was given when a person attacked or disrespected another person. The final offering was the Sin Offering. This offering was to be given by everybody, no exceptions. This was to cover ignorant or unintentional sins.

In Egypt the Israelites were property. They did as Pharaoh commanded, no questions asked. Their identity was found in Pharaoh. They didn't know anything else. They were born into it.

So, when God delivered them out of Egypt it was the perfect time to do some character building. They needed laws. They needed order. All they knew was their life in Egypt. That was their normal. At this point in time people were cruel and barbaric. Kings were worshiped as gods and they treated people as property. God needed to create a justice system. He needed to recreate order. So, He started with Israel.

NUMBERS AND DEUTERONOMY

While Leviticus begins with Moses standing outside of the Tabernacle, Numbers begins one month later with Moses inside the Tabernacle before God.

Numbers begins with a census of the generation of Israel that set out from Egypt, but interestingly the book was written to the generations to come. God was setting apart His people to become a nation. Before the people of Israel were to leave Sinai, they were going to know who they were and whom they represent.

> *The Lord also said to Moses, "I have taken the Levites from among the Israelites in place of the first male offspring of every Israelite woman. The Levites are mine, for all the firstborn are mine. When I struck down all the firstborn in Egypt, I set apart for myself every firstborn in Israel, whether human or animal. They are to be mine. I am the Lord." Numbers 3:11-13 NIV*

The Levites were set apart for God's holy priesthood. For the next several chapters God gave specific responsibilities for this group of people. The job description was anything but easy. There were specific laws and if you didn't follow them your life and job were at stake. They were *that* important.

The time was soon coming for the Israelites to set out for the Promised Land. They rested on this ground only months ago as a lost people running away from their past, but now they were running towards something—home.

The people of Israel observed the Passover and headed out. They packed up the entire camp including the entire tabernacle and courtyard furnishings. God guided them by pillar of cloud by day and pillar of fire by night. At the Lord's command the Israelites would journey and at His command they would camp.

> *Whenever the ark set out, Moses said, "Rise up, Lord! May your enemies be scattered; may your foes flee before you." Whenever it came to rest, he said, "Return, Lord, to the countless thousands of Israel." Numbers 10:35-36 NIV*

But it didn't take very long until the Israelites began to complain and God became angry. So angry that the fire of the Lord burned against them and consumed outer parts of the camp around them. The Israelites began to cry out, *Moses! Moses! Please stop this!* So Moses prayed to the Lord and the fire ceased.

Then the people cried out again in hunger and began to reminisce of all the foods they ate in Egypt. *Remember the fish? Oh, the fruit and vegetables! And it was all for free! But now all we have is this manna.*

God heard the Israelites cry, all right. But He wasn't happy. He had taken care of these people for months in the desert and yet they had seemed to forget! God was going to show them His power. He gathered Moses and the elders and told them that He was going to give them something different to eat. This time it was going to be meat. God was going to give them so much meat that it would come out of their nostrils (hopefully that was a metaphor).

Lord, where will you get this much meat? Moses began to ask. *There aren't enough flocks and herds and fish. There are six hundred thousand of us!* But God shot back, *is my power limited? Just sit back and watch me.*

God gave them so much meat that it was scattered three feet deep all around camp and took two entire days to gather. Oh, one more thing. The gathering was non-stop. They didn't sleep!

Maybe they got the message.

TWELVE SPIES. The Israelites moved on and finally arrived at their destination. They were so close yet all they needed was to trust God. But they were finally there. Oh the relief! Oh, the celebration!

They stood at the Jordan River overlooking the Promise Land and God gave them a command.

> *"Send some men to explore the land of Canaan, which I am giving to the Israelites. From each ancestral tribe send one of its leaders." Numbers 13:1-2 NIV*

See what the land is like.
Are the people strong or weak?
Few or many?
Rich or poor?
Is the land good or bad?
Are the towns fortified?
Bring back word of all you see!

> *At the end of forty days they returned from exploring the land. They came back to Moses and Aaron and the whole Israelite community at Kadesh in the Desert of Paran. There they reported to them and to the whole assembly and showed them the fruit of the land. They gave Moses this account: "We went into the land to which you sent us, and it does flow with milk and honey! Here is its fruit. But the people who live there are powerful, and*

the cities are fortified and very large. We even saw descendants of Anak there. The Amalekites live in the Negev; the Hittites, Jebusites and Amorites live in the hill country; and the Canaanites live near the sea and along the Jordan."

Then Caleb silenced the people before Moses and said, "We should go up and take possession of the land, for we can certainly do it." But the men who had gone up with him said, "We can't attack those people; they are stronger than we are." And they spread among the Israelites a bad report about the land they had explored. They said, "The land we explored devours those living in it. All the people we saw there are of great size." Numbers 13:25-32 NIV

Of course the people freaked out and chose not to go in.

This was supposed to be good! They were finally there! They'd been wandering for who knows how long and now this?

Moses and Aaron fell to the floor with their faces to the ground. Joshua and Caleb, two of the spies, spoke out to the crowd. *The land is good! It's flowing with milk and honey. If God is pleased with us He will deliver us and protect us as we go into the land. Do not rebel against God or fear the people of this land because God is with us!*

The Israelites were so lacking in confidence that they couldn't comprehend that this was possible. They couldn't understand that God was more powerful than their fears. Out of defiance they threatened to stone Joshua and Caleb.

Then God appeared to Moses at the Tent of Meeting (AKA the Tabernacle). *How long will this people despise me and not trust me? I've provided for them like children. I delivered them out of Egypt. I'm tired of their disobedience. I'll disinherit them and start over with you and make you into an even greater nation.*

But Moses interceded for the people. *Lord, the Egyptians saw your great might. They saw you lead us out of their country and they know you dwell with us. But what will they say if you kill your people in the wilderness? They would say you weren't mighty enough to deliver them into the land you have promised. Remember when you said,*

> *"The Lord is slow to anger, and abounding in steadfast love, forgiving iniquity and transgression"? (Numbers 14:18 NIV)*

Let your power be great in this way that you have promised. Forgive your people.

WANDERING. But the Lord's anger still burned. *I do forgive. But these people, though they've seen my glory, have tested me ten times and not obeyed me. None of those who have despised me will see the land that I have promised. Turn around tomorrow and set out for the wilderness by the way to the Red Sea. Tell the Israelites that I have heard their complaints against me. All those twenty years old and older who have complained against me shall not go into the land, except Joshua and Caleb. You will be shepherds in the wilderness for forty years because of your lack of faith, until the last of your dead bodies lies in the wilderness.*

So, what did the people do? They grumbled. *We have sinned against God, let's go into the land!* Moses commanded them not to because the Lord would not go with them. But what did they do? Some went anyway and were killed.

God then reminded Moses to spur on the people to follow His laws that He laid out for them. Some of the Israelites continued to rise up against God and they, along with their family, were destroyed.

God knew the Israelites had a way to go to become the mature and holy priesthood that He had called them to be. If it were God's way the Israelites would already be entering the land, but He needed the Israelites to be in a better place beforehand. The Israelites needed to desire the land that God had for them. But something within them still held on to Egypt. So the second generation of Israelites would be the ones to get an opportunity to prove themselves ready to enter the land and be the people God had called them to be.

But Moses wasn't finished yet. They continued to wander in the wilderness and battled anyone who got in their way.

BALAAM AND THE TALKING DONKEY. Along their journey Israel settled in the plains of Moab and their king became nervous. *They are more numerous and powerful than we are.* So the king summoned a prophet named Balaam.

Now Balaam was a pagan prophet. He worked for the gods and was internationally known. You might say a celebrity of that time. He was to the gods as Moses was to the one true God.

Balaam thought God was going to be easy to manipulate like the other gods. Boy, was he wrong. The king ordered Balaam to curse the nation of Israel (spiritual warfare in the Old Testament, am I right?). The king thought if he could battle Israel's God and win, they would no longer be a threat. But God spoke to Balaam and told him that his people were blessed and not to harm them. So, Balaam told the king's officials he wouldn't help him. But again, the king demanded Balaam to curse Israel. So, God told Balaam to follow the king's officials but to do what He commands him to do. Balaam saddled his donkey and set off with the officials. But he declared that he would not do anything beyond the word of God.

The angel of the Lord stood in the middle of the road where Balaam was riding and the donkey ran off the road in fear. But Balaam continued to try and gain control of his donkey by beating him several times before God opened its mouth and allowed it to talk. *What have I done to you to make you strike me this many times? I have been good to you!* (did this really just happen?) Then God spoke to Balaam telling him that his ways were perverse and that He had a plan for him.

Balaam arrived before the king of Moab where he was brought to speak curses onto the nation of Israel. But what came out of his mouth was a blessing!

The king was furious! He thought it was maybe their placement so he brought Balaam to another place that overlooked a portion of the people of Israel. But again, no curse! Only a blessing!

Balaam's eyes were then opened and seemed to finally understand who God was and so he stayed with God and uttered another blessing. The king was outraged!

Balaam reminded the king that when his officials summoned him, he told them that he would not go beyond the word of God. And again, Balaam spoke a blessing upon Israel!

BAD BLOOD. While camping out in Moab, the Israelites began to intermingle with Moabite women. Not only were they sleeping with them, but they were also taking part in their worship and eating their foods.

The people who were called to be set apart were acting like the rest of the world. The Israelites were resorting back to a similar way of life they had lived in Egypt. Though they were experiencing a new healthy way of life, it was easier to go back to what they once knew. The Lord plagued those that disobeyed Him and purged the people.

The Lord then demanded that Moses and the priest take a new census of people and to introduce new laws to prepare the people for their soon inheritance of the Promised Land! After taking the census, not one person of the first generation of Israel delivered out of Egypt was alive, except Moses, Joshua and Caleb.

Moses, the (mostly) righteous man we have followed for a good while, had grown old. His life was coming to an end and his role needed to be filled before the people could enter into the Promised Land. And who was it that would lead the people? None other than Joshua, son of Nun.

Now to the land flowing with milk and honey.

PART THREE
Back to the Promised Land

JOSHUA

CHAPTER NINE

As I was with Moses, so I will be with you; I will never leave you nor forsake you. Joshua 1:5-6 NIV

WE'RE FINALLY HERE

Have you ever worked for someone and hoped that one day you would be lucky enough to have their job? Maybe if you put in enough hours, took enough online courses, befriended enough coworkers, the job could become yours?

I grew up in a church youth group that luckily had two fantastic youth ministers who poured greatly into me. After I graduated from college with a degree in Bible, those same youth ministers hired me as their apprentice at the church where they were working. After graduate school, it came time for me to get my own gig and the church I grew up at hired me to be their new youth minister; which is where I am now. Long story short, I now have the job that my previous youth ministers had. I work in the same office they did when they poured into me as a teenager. Now, I get to pour into my teens.

Joshua, son of Nun (How cool is that name?), was Moses' aid for many years during the wandering and now he wasn't the aid anymore - he was The Guy. But this job didn't come without a job description.

> *Moses my servant is dead. Now then, you and all these people, get ready to cross the Jordan River into the land I am about to give to them—to the Israelites. I will give you every place where you set your foot, as I promised Moses. Your territory will extend from the desert to Lebanon, and from the great river, the Euphrates—all the Hittite country— to the Mediterranean Sea in the west. No one will be able to stand against you all the days of your life. As I was with Moses, so I will be with you; I will never leave you nor forsake you. Be strong and courageous, because you will lead these people to inherit the land I swore to their ancestors to give them.*
>
> *Be strong and very courageous. Be careful to obey all the law my servant Moses gave you; do not turn from it to the right or to the left, that you may be successful wherever you go. Keep this Book of the Law always on your lips; meditate on it day and night, so that you may be careful to do everything written in it. Then you will be prosperous and successful. Have I not commanded you? Be strong and courageous. Do not be afraid; do not be discouraged, for the Lord your God will be with you wherever you go." Joshua 1:2-9 NIV*

Joshua had a lot on his plate. But to know that God was on your side and willing to fight alongside you to protect you, that's a pretty neat feeling.

Joshua commanded the officers of Israel to prepare to cross the Jordan River in three days. What Israel had been awaiting for many years was three days away.

Have you ever had to wait for something that you *really* wanted? I mean *really* wanted. A home? A job? A cure? The gift that God had promised the Israelites was a stone's throw away from them and they were soon to set foot in this land.

But, the thing about this land was . . . It was occupied. There were villages of people living across the entire land. So Joshua sent two spies ahead of them to view the land. Did you notice this time two spies were sent instead of twelve like the last time? Maybe Joshua remembered what it was like to be outnumbered last time.

RAHAB THE PROSTITUTE. Immediately after we're told the spies were sent out, we're told that they enter into the house of a prostitute. This is the first thing the Israelites do once they set foot in the land they've been awaiting for so many years? God had been grooming this people to be a nation of priests and this is how they act?

King! King! Two men have snuck into town and they're searching out the land! We saw them enter Rahab's home!

Word was out! The king sent some of his men to her house to get rid of them, but Rahab hid the spies on her roof and told the king's men that they had moved on.

Do you know what happened next?

Rahab began to pour her heart out to the spies. *I know that God has given your people this land. We've heard how God dried up the Red Sea for you to cross out of Egypt. We've heard how mighty your God is and that He fights for you. Your God is indeed the true God. Since I have been good to you, promise me that you will spare my family and me!*

The spies gave her their word. *Tie a red cord in your window and keep all of your family inside your home and you will be spared.*

The two spies made it back safely to Joshua and gave word: *Truly God has given us this land; the people melt in fear before us. They've heard all that God has done for us!*

CROSSING THE JORDAN. Early in the morning Joshua and all the Israelites set out from Shittim and went to the Jordan, where they camped before crossing over. After three days the officers went throughout the camp, giving orders to the people: "When you see the ark of the covenant of the Lord your God, and the Levitical priests carrying it, you are to move out from your positions and follow it. Then you will know which way to go, since you have never been this way before. But keep a distance of about two thousand cubits between you and the ark; do not go near it."

Joshua told the people, "Consecrate yourselves, for tomorrow the Lord will do amazing things among you."

Joshua said to the priests, "Take up the ark of the covenant and pass on ahead of the people." So they took it up and went ahead of them.

And the Lord said to Joshua, "Today I will begin to exalt you in the eyes of all Israel, so they may know that I am with you as I was with Moses. Tell the

> *priests who carry the ark of the covenant: 'When you reach the edge of the Jordan's waters, go and stand in the river.'" Joshua 3:1-8 NIV*

Do you feel the movement? God was then leading the people from the Ark of the Covenant rather than by cloud or pillar of fire. God now resided within the camp. Throughout the story of the Bible, be looking for God as He continues to move closer and closer to His people.

The time had come for all of Israel to cross the Jordan River and step foot onto the land that God had gifted them.

> *The priests who carried the ark of the covenant of the Lord stopped in the middle of the Jordan and stood on dry ground, while all Israel passed by until the whole nation had completed the crossing on dry ground. Joshua 3:17 NIV*

As soon as the priest's feet touched the waters of the Jordan, water was cut off on either side of them. Does this remind you of crossing the Red Sea? Exactly! Through small and big events God was continually illustrating that He is distinct from the other gods. He is real and He is powerful.

The significance of this is God's presence. The placement of the ark revealed God's presence before them, in their midst and behind them. God was dwelling among the Israelites and providing them protection on all sides. This expedition was going to change the Israelites' lives forever and God was there for every step of it. In this story we see God as a protective father carrying the people home after they had been lost for so many years.

The tribes of Rueben, Gad and Manasseh crossed the Jordan in full gear, ready for battle, as Moses had commanded them before his death. Forty thousand armed for battle crossed the river that day. God's people were armed and ready.

After crossing, Joshua set up twelve stones in the middle of the Jordan as a memorial of God's deliverance.

On the fourth day after crossing the Jordan, the Israelites celebrated the Sabbath. On this day the manna ceased. No longer were the people living in the past of their ancestors and their judgment. They could now eat crops from their land. Gift accepted.

Can you imagine how good it felt to be home? Although they were still camping out on the road, they were finally in the land that they had longed for. They were one step closer to being a nation. They were soon to own their own land. They were about to have their own houses. If you've ever owned your own home, you know how it feels to get the keys to it, walk into it knowing it's yours. This was the stage of excitement the Israelites were experiencing.

But there was some work to do before the land was all theirs.

OCCUPY THE LAND. Other people were currently occupying the land that Israel was being given. It wasn't just one nation to take over though. Israel needed to destroy the many nations occupying the land. There were even rules God gave them about how they were to properly do it.

Every living thing and all idols were to be destroyed.

All silver, gold, bronze and iron were sacred to God and were to be put in the treasury of the Lord.

God had just rescued His people from Egypt and was finally getting them to become somewhat closer to the holy nation He envisioned them to be.

They were not to intermarry anyone from that land. The nations that were living in the land were considered defiled by God and were to be killed. The people as a whole were so lost that God didn't want them to influence the rest of the world.

So Israel went to war and God was with them.

JERICHO. First stop, Jericho. God commanded the Israelites to march seven times around the wall of the city and then blow their trumpets and the wall fell down. The two spies ran to Rahab's house to spare them from destruction and they were to be the only things taken from Jericho. Everything else was condemned to destruction.

But one man named Achan became in awe of what he saw in Jericho. He saw gold and silver and riches! So he stole some of it thinking no one would notice.

AI. Feeling pretty good about themselves, Israel went to war with another city nearby called Ai. They were smaller than Jericho and things were going well until Ai started killing Israel's men! *Retreat! Retreat!* Joshua tore his clothes and fell to the ground before the ark of the Lord. *God, why have you brought us here to be destroyed? What have we done to deserve this?* But God replied,

> "Stand up! What are you doing down on your face? Israel has sinned; they have violated my

> *covenant, which I commanded them to keep. They have taken some of the devoted things; they have stolen, they have lied, they have put them with their own possessions. That is why the Israelites cannot stand against their enemies; they turn their backs and run because they have been made liable to destruction. I will not be with you anymore unless you destroy whatever among you is devoted to destruction. Go, consecrate the people. Tell them, 'consecrate yourselves in preparation for tomorrow; for this is what the Lord, the God of Israel, says: There are devoted things among you, Israel. You cannot stand against your enemies until you remove them.'" Joshua 7:10-13 NIV*

The next morning Joshua called the clans of the Tribe of Judah forward family by family (Achan had to have been sweating). After calling several family leaders, Joshua called Achan to come forward. He quickly admitted to his sin but that didn't mean he wasn't punished for his wrongdoing. If there was a bad time to sin, it was then. God was making a distinction between Israel and the defiled people living in the land, and the second you begin to look more like the defiled than the called . . . you will be taken care of. The people stoned Achan and his family as a warning to the rest of the people. *Follow the rules. You are set apart.*

Once the stolen items were taken from Achan the Israelites went back to fight the city of Ai and won. Then Joshua built an altar renewing Israel's covenant to God and read the Book of the Law to Israel. That's right, the first five books of the Bible that we just finished reading about: Genesis; Exodus; Leviticus; Numbers and Deuteronomy, Joshua read to the people.

(Side Note: Mount Ebal is in Shechem. This is the place that Abraham was first given the gift of the land for his descendants. Now the Israelites were finally back home!)

But they were still in a war zone.
God had been doing some pretty incredible things and it didn't take long for the neighboring nations to hear about it and decided to join forces to attack Israel.

First, the Gibeonites who lived nearby decided to trick Israel into making a treaty with them by telling Joshua that they were from a distant land and had heard of God's mighty hand. It didn't go very well for the people of Gibeon because they were cursed and placed as slaves for Israel, but I guess that's better for them than their entire people being killed.

Then, there was a battle where the sun literally stood still.

Yes, you read that right.

The king of Jerusalem was alarmed because he got wind of all the defeats Israel had under their belt. Not only did they escape Egypt, defeat Jericho, Ai, among some other groups along the way . . . they had made treaty with the people of Gibeon. Gibeon was an important city. Not only was it important, but also a royal city. And they were very skilled fighters.

Then the king of Jerusalem made a pact with the kings of Hebron, Jarmuth, Lachish and Eglon. They were going to wage war together on Gibeon to knock the legs out from under Israel. So without Gibeon they might stand a chance against Israel.

(Side Note: This is the same Hebron that Abraham had lived and where he, Isaac, Jacob and their wives were buried.)

Gibeon told Joshua what these kings were going to do and Joshua grabbed all of his fighting men and took off for an all night journey to Gibeon to catch them by surprise. Before the big battle God spoke to Joshua,

> "Do not be afraid of them; I have given them into your hand. Not one of them will be able to withstand you." Joshua 10:8 NIV

Then Joshua prayed to the Lord.

> "Sun, stand still over Gibeon, and you, moon, over the Valley of Aijalon." So the sun stood still, and the moon stopped, till the nation avenged itself on its enemies. Joshua 10:12-13 NIV

With God by their side, Israel killed many of their men. They chased their armies out of Gibeon and God threw large hailstones on them killing even more of them than Israel did with swords.

But the kings feared for their lives and hid in a cave. When Israel got word, they brought the men before Joshua where he killed them. The surrounding nations didn't utter a word against Israel for they feared for their lives.

After all this, Joshua turned to the Israelites,

> "Do not be afraid; do not be discouraged. Be strong and courageous. This is what the Lord will

> do to all the enemies you are going to fight." Joshua 10:25 NIV

Joshua led the Israelites to conquer Kingdoms all over Canaan. Not one city, except for the Gibeonites, made it out alive.

When Joshua had grown old, the Lord spoke to him.

> *"You are now very old, and there are still very large areas of land to be taken over." Joshua 13:1 NIV.*

After the Israelites had been in the land for an extended period of time, God nudged them to take over the rest of the land that He prepared for them. This was the area of the Philistines: Gaza, Ashdod, Ashkelon, Gath and Ekron, along with Phoenicia and Lebanon over to Mount Hermon.

Joshua then divided up the land among the tribes and the people began to settle for the first time in their own villages. The people were finally home.

Joshua only gets one book in the Bible, yet he does some pretty incredible things. He is mentioned in the books of Moses as his aid, but in the book of Joshua we really get a sense that he was truly an incredible leader. He took a group of people who felt like property to become a mighty nation. We call them Israel, but they still saw themselves on many levels as property of Egypt at the beginning of Joshua. Finally we start to see them view themselves as God's people.

Take notice, these men were not fighters. They were wanderers. They were a scattered people who were in the middle of searching for who they truly were. God took that group of people and turned them into a mighty army of the Lord. And it was through this people that God was going to redeem the world.

JOSHUA'S FAREWELL. *My death is coming soon. You have seen all the wonders God has performed in front of you. He has followed through on all His promises. Now you, continue to follow the Law of Moses. Do not be influenced by your surrounding nations or by their gods. If you do, God will not fight for you any longer. If you violate God's commandments you will surely perish from this promised land God has gifted us.*

Joshua's story ends with him reminding Israel of their story of deliverance. Then he asked the people who they would serve. Would it be God or the gods of other nations? Israel shouted in one accord, *We will serve the Lord!*

In one final charge he held the people accountable for their commitment and demanded them to rid their cities of all foreign gods. It was there in the city of Shechem that Joshua made one last covenant between the people and God that they would serve the Lord and obey Him.

And just like that, Joshua's time had come and he was buried in the land that he had inherited.

> *Israel served the Lord throughout the lifetime of Joshua and of the elders who outlived him and who had experienced everything the Lord had done for Israel. Joshua 24:31 NIV*

Now, who was going to lead the people?

JUDGES
CHAPTER TEN

Then the Lord raised up judges, who saved them out of the hands of these raiders. Judges 2:16 NIV

The book of Joshua brought the people into the Promised Land. But Judges illustrates the cycle of depravity that brought the people down again and again and again once they settled there. In the death of Joshua, the Israelites lost their direction. When that generation died, another generation grew up that hadn't seen God's miraculous wonders and lost sight of Him.

There were still people living in the Promised Land that Israel had yet to defeat, and they struggled to defeat them. They began worshiping the gods of the surrounding people and God was righteously angry. So He gave the Israelites into the hands of their enemies because of their sin. But this was what Joshua told them would happen. He warned them not to follow the gods of the people around them or God would not fight for them.

When Israel got desperate enough, God raised up judges over Israel to lead them.

OTHNIEL. The Israelites cried out for help in their desperation. They worshiped other gods, but when push came to shove, those gods didn't respond. God, caught between anger and fatherly love, raised up a judge to save His people.

Our God responds.

God chose Othniel, Caleb's nephew (one of the original twelve spies), to fight for Israel and take Joshua's place. The Spirit of the Lord came on Othniel and God began to fight for Israel again. There was peace in the land for forty years! But, then Othniel died. And guess what?

EHUD. The people began to do evil in the eyes of the Lord.

Is this thing on repeat?

God stopped fighting for Israel and King Eglon of Moab, along with the Ammonites and Amalekites, attacked Israel! They took possession of Jericho! It began to look like the conquest that Joshua had pursued was being reversed. So, of course, they cried out to God again and He placed another judge over Israel and this guy's name was Ehud.

He was left-handed.

Why was that fact important? Let's take a step back for a second. When you're reading the Bible and something seems absurd, look deeper. Dwell there.

Ehud visited King Eglon to deliver a gift. A gift to the enemy? He strapped a double-edged sword to his right thigh under his clothing. Ehud told the king that he had a secret message to deliver. So the king cleared the room.

Ehud approached the king as he edged closer to hear the message. Pulling the sword out from his side he plunged it into the king's belly. Now, this king was a very large man. So large that the sword, and even its handle, was swallowed up by the fat that closed in around it.

The significance? God chose a left-handed man in a predominantly right-handed world to do something extravagant. No one would check the right thigh of a man for a sword, for men are right handed and would place them in a holster on the left thigh for quick ease to grab and fight. What's even more significant? God always wins.

> That day Moab was made subject to Israel, and the land had peace for eighty years. Judges 3:30 NIV

SAHMGAR. *After Ehud came Shamgar son of Anath, who struck down six hundred Philistines with an oxgoad. He too saved Israel. Judges 3:31 NIV*

Oxgoad, huh? Shamgar took a utensil that was used to urge an ox to continue working to kill six hundred Philistines. You know Goliath? Yeah, he was a Philistine.

DEBORAH. But, after Ehud and Shamgar . . . the Israelites still hadn't learned their lesson. They began to do evil in the eyes of the Lord, again! So God sold them into the hands of the king of Canaan in Hazor where they were oppressed for twenty years. They cried out to the Lord, and of course He listened. God hears us when we talk to Him, even when we're deceitful.

During this time a prophet named Deborah was leading Israel. The Israelites brought their disputes before her and she judged over them.

God told Deborah to summon ten thousand men of the tribe of Naphtali and Zebulun to overtake Canaan and their army commander Sisera. So she grabbed Barak from the tribe of Naphtali to assemble their men at once. But Barak jumped back in his seat. *I will go if you do, but not if you don't!* Agreeing to the terms Deborah shot back,

> "Certainly I will go with you. But because of the course you are taking, the honor will not be yours, for the Lord will deliver Sisera into the hands of a woman." Judges 4:9 NIV

Deborah shouted, *Go! This is the day the Lord has given Sisera into your hands!* The men were ready for battle. Everything was in place. God routed Sisera and his men right into the hands of Israel's fighting men. It was a bloodfest. Sisera hopped off his chariot and ran! He ran right into the tent of Jael, the wife of a man named Heber, because Canaan had an alliance with this family.

But less about the family alliance or even about who Jael was married to. This was all about something more. Jael picked up a tent peg and drove it right through Sisera's head! It was a woman who slayed the army of Canaan and it was a woman who was leading the people of Israel.

Barak looked everywhere for Sisera and came to Jael's tent in pursuit of him. Jael invited Barak into her tent to show him their victory.

> On that day God subdued Jabin king of Canaan before the Israelites. And the hand of the Israelites pressed harder and harder against Jabin king of Canaan until they destroyed him. Judges 4:23-24 NIV

GIDEON. But, yet again Israel did evil in the eyes of the Lord. So God gave them into the hands of the Midianites as a consequence. These people were different. They were so oppressive that the Israelites hid in caves and shelters. As they grew crops, the Midianites would take them. As they raised livestock, the Midiaites would steal them. Nothing living was left for the Israelites. They became so poor and famished that they finally turned to God for help in their crying.

> "I brought you up out of Egypt, out of the land of slavery. I rescued you from the hand of the Egyptians. And I delivered you from the hand of all your oppressors; I drove them out before you and gave you their land. I said to you, 'I am the Lord your God; do not worship the gods of the Amorites, in whose land you live.' But you have not listened to me." Judges 6:8-10 NIV

Then the angel of the Lord appeared before a man named Gideon. He was a common man, much like us. *The Lord is with you, mighty warrior.* In hearing this, Gideon was taken aback. *If God is with us why is all of this bad stuff happening to us? What happened to all of the wonders our ancestors had told us about. But now He has abandoned us and given us over to the Midianites.*

But God turned to Gideon and told him that He had strengthened him and was sending him to save Israel. *But I am the weakest of my family and our clan is the weakest of our tribe!* But God promised Gideon that with Him they would win and there would be no survivor from the Midianites.

Can you imagine being Gideon? You've heard of God all your life. Your people are in gut wrenching persecution and then, poof, there He is, God almighty right in front of you.

So Gideon asked God to prove that He was who He said He was. But first Gideon wanted to bring an offering before Him. So, Gideon asks God to wait. What? Yes, an average dude asked God to hold on a second and He did. So he ran back to the house, grabbed some unleavened bread, a young goat and its broth and returned to God (thanks for holding!). The angel of God then told Gideon to set the food on a rock and the rock set ablaze with fire and was consumed. After seeing this, Gideon couldn't believe his eyes and knew it was the Lord!

God then told Gideon to tear down his father's altar to the god Baal and Asherah pole and to build a proper altar to Him; the one true God. And then offer a sacrifice.

But the morning brought chaos. The people demanded to know who tore down Baal's altar and the Asherah pole. The Israelites wanted to kill Gideon when they found out it was him! But Gideon's father exclaimed,

> *"Are you going to plead Baal's cause? Are you trying to save him? Whoever fights for him shall be put to death by morning! If Baal really is a god, he can defend himself when someone breaks down his altar." Judges 6:31 NIV*

About this time the Midianites, Amalekites and other eastern nations joined forces to attack Israel, but the Spirit of the Lord came on Gideon! Freeing himself of any doubt, Gideon asked God for a couple more miracles to prove that God was on his side. Of course God pulled through.

Gideon grabbed his army of men and placed them into a position that would challenge their enemy, but God stopped Gideon. *You have too many men. Israel will think they saved themselves. Anyone that is fearful, tell them to turn back.* So Gideon did so and twenty-two thousand men left, leaving ten thousand behind to fight.

So again, ready for battle, God pulled Gideon aside. *There are just still too many men. Take them down to get water. Separate those who drink like a dog from those who kneel to drink.* Gideon went through with it and found three hundred men drinking like dogs.

Them! I will use them! Send everyone else home!

Gideon was blindsided. The ones that lapped up their water with their tongues like dogs? You want to use them?

God reassured Gideon that He would deliver the Midianites into his hands. But just in case Gideon was still nervous, God told him to go down and spy out the people and listen to what they were saying. So Gideon and his servant went down to the camp. They heard two people talking. A man was telling his friend about a dream he had and the friend interpreted it as the Israelites defeating them. When Gideon heard the dream's interpretation, he could only fall to knees and worship God!

> *"Get up! The Lord has given the Midianite camp into your hands." Judges 7:15 NIV*

Gideon split the men into three groups placing trumpets and empty jars with torches inside into each of their hands.
Follow my lead! When I, and those with me, get to the edge of camp and blow our trumpets you will blow yours and then shout, "FOR THE LORD AND FOR GIDEON!"

After Gideon reached the edge of camp the Midianite guards were changing their guards. Gideon and his men blew their trumpets then the rest of the men broke their jars revealing the flames and blew their trumpets! And then shouted, "A SWORD FOR THE LORD AND FOR GIDEON!"

The camp went wild. People were running into each other. No one knew where to run. God threw the people into confusion and they began to turn on each other. All this while Gideon and his men held their positions. The tribes of Naphtali, Asher and Manasseh who were sent home were all called out to pursue the Midianites.

To finish the battle, Gideon killed the two kings of Midian.

The people pleaded with Gideon and his sons to lead the nation of Israel, but Gideon refused their offer. *You do not serve me. You serve the Lord!* In most cases, Israel would take goods from the nations they demolished. And so they did with Midian. Gideon made the people give up gold earrings and he formed them into a priestly garment to offer a portion of their plunder to God. Not long after the garment was made Gideon and the people began to worship it and were led back into idolatry.

During Gideon's lifetime the nation experienced peace for forty years. Gideon grew old in age and died and the people resorted back to Baal. They forgot God and Gideon despite all the good they had done.

ABIMELEK. Now, the Israelites were still acting terrible and Abimelek, one of Gideon's sons, had a thirst for control. He went before his mother's clan in Shechem and pleaded with them to make him king.

The people agreed that Abimelek was a good fit . . . and he was family. They gave him money from the temple of their gods and Abimelek hired some followers.

(Doesn't that set up well for a leader? Hire people who listen to you)

He then went to his father's house and killed all of his brothers except one, the youngest brother Jotham, who managed to get away. He wanted to be the only heir to the throne.

As the people of Shechem gathered to crown Abimelek as king, Jotham stood atop a mountain to persuade the people.

Listen to me . . . so that God may listen to you! He then recited a poem illustrating trees going out to anoint a king over themselves. An olive tree, fig tree and vine all rejected the invitation of kingly duties saying they were designed to bear fruit. They understood their design and function. The poem ends with the trees seeking out kingship in a thorn bush in their desperation.

In other words, *you're crowning my brother because you can't find a better option? Bad idea! Come on, people!*

And then we watch as Jotham flees for his life. Abimelek sadly took the throne and served three years.

But this story doesn't end that quickly.

God didn't just sit still. He was angry with Abimelek and how he acted against his family so He stirred up the city of Shechem against Abimelek.

Then a man named Gaal moved into town. The people began to look to him instead of Abimelek! Gaal was pretty hot headed from the start and challenged Shechem's allegiance. *Why serve Abimelek and not Shechem's father, Hamor? If you people were in my command I would get rid of him!*

So what happened next? Zebul, Abimelek's right hand man, heard what Gaal had been saying and reported it to Abimelek. Abimelek and his men went out at dark to attack Gaal's people. He tried desperately to defend himself but Abimelek and his men chased them and killed many of his people. Then they destroyed the city and burned one thousand people alive hiding in a tower. Talk about gore.

> *Next Abimelek went to [the city of] Thebez and besieged it and captured it. Inside the city, however, was a strong tower, to which all the people of the city had fled. They had locked themselves in and climbed up on the tower roof. Abimelek went to the tower and attacked it. But as he approached the entrance to the tower to set it on fire, a woman dropped an upper millstone on his head and cracked his skull. Hurriedly he called to his armor-bearer, "Draw your sword and kill me, so that they can't say, 'A woman killed him.'" Judges 9:50-54 NIV*

God repaid Abimelek and Shechem for their wickedness with death. And God even took it a step further with Abimelek and added the element of embarrassment! After Abimelek's death the Israelite army scattered and returned home. Thus Israel's first attempt at kingship was a disaster.

TOLA. Abimelek only reigned a measly three years (which is okay with me). But Tola took the reins and lead the nation for twenty-three years! The scriptures states that he rose to save Israel! This longevity would have allowed Tola to redirect the people into back into a royal priesthood.

JAIR. After Tola, Israel had another judge who had a good run. Jair judged over Israel for twenty-two years. From what we read in scripture, Jair continued Tola's good work.

JEPHTHAH. But again, Israel did evil in the eyes of the Lord. They began worshiping the gods of the surrounding peoples and God became angry. So what did He do? He sold them to the Philistines and Ammonites. For eighteen years the Israelites were oppressed.

So Israel did what they do best when they don't get their way. They cried out to God for deliverance. *We have sinned against you! Forgive us!* But God didn't save them. Instead He told Israel to cry out to the other gods they were so determined to praise. Ouch!

Did you catch that? God provided. Yet Israel praised the gods that didn't provide them anything.

Have you ever given a gift to someone and they thanked someone else for it? Of course not! How would you feel? YOU put effort into finding the perfect gift. Yet that didn't seem to matter to Israel when it came to God. They turned elsewhere nearly every time.

Israel continued to cry out to God:

> "We have sinned. Do with us whatever you think best, but please rescue us now." Then they got rid of the foreign gods among them and served the Lord. And he could bear Israel's misery no longer. Judges 10:15-16 NIV

He could bear Israel's misery no longer. Wow. God's love for Israel overcame their punishment. Sound familiar, parents?

But who would lead the people since Jair had passed away?

Jephthah! A mighty warrior with an awkward family history. He was the love child of a one-night stand, living with his father, stepmother and half-brothers. To keep their father's inheritance to themselves the brothers drove Jephthah away. He was a misfit. But God is good at using misfits to do unimaginably great things.

Years later, Jephthah's brothers begged him to move back to lead them in battle against the Ammonites. After some convincing, he was Israel's guy and hopped right to the job. His first line of duty was to speak with the king of Ammon to seek peace. But that didn't go so well and he declared war on Israel. Jephthah was good at his job but he knew he wouldn't stand a chance without God on his side.

As Israel advanced against Ammon, Jephthah made a vow to God:

JUDGES

> *"If you give the Ammonites into my hands, whatever comes out of the door of my house to meet me when I return in triumph from the Ammonites will be the Lord's, and I will sacrifice it as a burnt offering."*
> *Judges 11:30-31 NIV*

God kept His end of the deal and delivered the Ammonites into Jephthah's hands. But when he returned home from war his daughter walked out to greet him.

It was in an instant that he remembered his vow. He tore his clothes and cried because he knew breaking his vow with God was worse than losing his only child.

All in all, Jephthah led Israel for six years and then he died.

IBZAN. Up until this point, most of Israel's judges were from the north. But Ibzan came from the city of Bethlehem, near Jerusalem. He led the people of Israel for seven years.

ELON. After Ibzan came Elon and he led Israel for ten years. This guy, perhaps, gets the shortest description of all the judges in scripture.

ABDON. Elon passed the torch on to Abdon in his death and he led Israel for eight years. This guy was wealthy. He had forty sons and thirty grandsons along with seventy donkeys.

SAMSON. But, sadly again Israel did evil in the eyes of the Lord. So He delivered them into the hands of the Philistines for forty years.

By this point God had already rose up eleven judges (and one self-proclaimed king) to rule over Israel. Would this vicious cycle of depravity ever end? Who would God raise up this time?

Now, there was a woman in the tribe of Dan who could not conceive a child with her husband. An angel of the Lord came to her and said,

> *"You are barren and childless, but you are going to become pregnant and give birth to a son. Now see to it that you drink no wine or other fermented drink and that you do not eat anything unclean. You will become pregnant and have a son whose head is never to be touched by a razor because the boy is to be a Nazirite, dedicated to God from the womb. He will take the lead in delivering Israel from the hands of the Philistines." Judges 13:3-5 NIV*

A Nazarite vow was one of holiness and being set apart. God knew His people; they needed someone set apart from their ways. The sin cycle needed to be broken. But can you imagine waiting for this fetus to grow into a man who would lead the nation out of turmoil?

I love how God works miracles in the lives of couples that struggle to conceive. This isn't always the case for all women, but I love how God uses such a delicate situation to bring forth something beautiful into the world.

As Samson grew into manhood his eyes were set upon a young Philistine woman who he wanted to take as his wife. His parents forbade it but that didn't seem to stop him. He thought maybe if he married into the Philistine nation he would have a better opportunity to infiltrate and overcome the Philistines.

On his way to find this woman, a lion attacked him and the Spirit of the Lord rushed into Samson and he tore the lion apart. Samson grew to be somewhat of a Biblical Hercules.

Samson's strength won himself many attacks against the Philistines, but probably the most famous of all is found in Judges Chapter fifteen. After Samson had set fire to the Philistines' grain and olive orchards in retribution for a previous ploy, the Philistines were out to kill Samson. They searched out Samson in the town of Judah where the Judeans tied up Samson and delivered him to the enemy. But things didn't end very well for the Philistines.

> *The Spirit of the Lord came powerfully upon him. The ropes on his arms became like burnt flax, and the bindings melted from his hands. Finding a fresh jawbone of a donkey, he grabbed it and struck down a thousand men. Judges 15:14-15 NIV*

In spite of God's explicit direction to fight the Philistines, we find Samson falling in love all over again with someone outside of Israel. Yet another Philistine woman, the notorious Delilah.

Samson's strength was no secret; but the source of that strength became a question for the Philistines. So they tasked Delilah to find out his secret.

Delilah begged Samson three times to know the source of his strength, but three times Samson lied to her. After nagging him over and over again he couldn't take it anymore. And just like that the secret was out.

> *"No razor has ever been used on my head," he said, "because I have been a Nazirite dedicated*

> *to God from my mother's womb. If my head were shaved, my strength would leave me." Judges 16:17 NIV*

As he fell asleep, Delilah took a razor and shaved off his hair and immediately God's power left him. Delilah handed him over to the Philistines and they gouged out his eyes and placed him in prison. The world's once strongest man was left blind and weak.

But the story wasn't over.

The Philistines took Samson down to Gaza to make him a laughing stock to the Philistines. They mocked him for his allegiance to God and bound him between two pillars.

But God should never be mocked.

In one final act, God sent Samson a burst of strength. He pushed against the pillars and brought down the entire temple killing himself and all those inside with him.

> *Thus he killed many more when he died than while he lived. Judges 16:30 NIV*

SAMUEL. There was a certain man named Elkanah who had two wives, Hannah and Peninnah. Peninnah had children but Hannah could not conceive.

> *Year after year this man went up from his town to worship and sacrifice to the Lord Almighty at Shiloh, where Hophni and Phinehas, the two sons of Eli, were priests of the Lord. 1 Samuel 1:3 NIV*

When the day came for Elkanah to take his family to Shiloh for their sacrifice, he would give portions of the meat to Peninnah and for her sons but he would give a double portion to Hannah because he loved her. But Hannah's pain overcame her to the point of weeping. Elkanah tried to comfort her but nothing could stop the pain.

Hannah began praying to God for a miracle.

> "Lord Almighty, if you will only look on your servant's misery and remember me, and not forget your servant but give her a son, then I will give him to the Lord for all the days of his life, and no razor will ever be used on his head." 1 Samuel 1:11 NIV

Eli stood nearby, hearing Hannah's suffering and blessed her.

Early the next morning Hannah and her husband woke up and worshiped God. Then they went back home and made love. But God didn't forget Hannah's prayer. She became pregnant and gave birth to a son and named him Samuel.

Hannah's prayer was not only for a son. She prayed fervently for a God-fearing son. No razor was to touch his head signifying that he was to be a Nazarite.

> The Lord was with Samuel as he grew up, and he let none of Samuel's words fall to the ground. And all Israel from Dan to Beersheba recognized that Samuel was attested as a prophet of the Lord. 1 Samuel 3:19-20 NIV

The Philistines continued to pursue Israel even after Samson's death. During one mission, they stole the Ark of the Covenant from Israel and placed it in their temple to the god of Dagon. Each morning they would find their statue of Dagon broken and on its knees before the Ark. How cool is that? The people thought if they captured the Ark they would hold the power of Israel's God. Boy, were they wrong! As long as they kept it their people were struck with tumors and devastation. Finally, it was returned to its place in Israel and they defeated the Philistines.

WE WANT A KING. When Samuel grew old, he appointed his sons as Israel's leader. But, his sons did not follow his ways. They turned aside after dishonest gain and accepted bribes and perverted justice.

So all the elders of Israel gathered together and came to Samuel. They said to him, "You are old, and your sons do not follow your ways; now appoint a king to lead us, **such as all the other nations have.**"

But when they said, "Give us a king to lead us," this displeased Samuel; so he prayed to the Lord. And the Lord told him: "Listen to all that the people are saying to you; **it is not you they have rejected, but they have rejected me as their king.** *As they have done from the day I brought them up out of Egypt until this day, forsaking me and serving other gods, so they are doing to you." 1 Samuel 8:1-8 NIV*

God gave Samuel words to bring back to Israel. *This king you ask for will have high demands! He will take of your harvest, cattle, flocks, servants, and you yourselves will become slaves. When you have a king you will cry out for relief but I, the Lord, will not answer you.*

But the people refused to listen . . . we want a king!

. . . so God gave them a king.

PART FOUR
Do Good

KINGS

CHAPTER ELEVEN

Now appoint a king to lead us, such as all the other nations have. 1 Samuel 8:5 NIV

Then what you have in 1 and 2 Samuel, 1 and 2 Kings, and then repeated again in 1 and 2 Chronicles is the movement from the period of the judges to Israel's kingship.

RUTH

Before we go any further, there's a woman that we need to talk about.

Before Israel had a king, God was already forming a lineage much greater than the king that Israel had asked for. This lineage had great purpose.

There was a great famine in the land and a certain man named Elimelek, his wife Naomi and their two boys left their home in Bethlehem for the country of Moab to find food.

(Side note: Bethlehem means "House of Bread" yet they lacked food.)

Once they arrived at their new home, Elimelek died. He fled to save his families lives but in doing so lost his own. Their two sons then married Moabite women and they died! So there you go, Naomi and her two daughters-in-law, Orpah and Ruth, were left widowed to fend for themselves.

(Side note: Moab was outside of Israelite territory and therefore Elimelek deserted his native country for the idolatrous Moab. AKA, Elimelek deserted God. His boys followed suit by marrying Moabite women.)

Naomi heard that God had provided for Israel amidst the famine and decided to go back home. She packed up her family's luggage and left for Judah. Then she looked at her sons' wives and told them to go back to their mothers' homes. *I am old and you have so much life to live. Go back to your families and find new husbands!* But the girls wouldn't listen and wanted to go with Naomi. Orpah gave in and returned home but Ruth wouldn't leave Naomi's side.

> *"Don't urge me to leave you or to turn back from you. Where you go I will go, and where you stay I will stay. Your people will be my people and your God my God" Ruth 1:16 NIV*

Naomi and Ruth were dirt poor. Once they arrived in Bethlehem, Ruth would go out to the fields behind the harvesters and take from the leftover grain for her and

Naomi to eat. She began to glean in the field of Boaz who happened to be her father-in-law's relative (and who also happened to find her very attractive).

Ruth, don't glean in another field but stay here and I will care for you. Drink from my water and eat from my foods.

Boaz took such great care of Ruth that Naomi knew without a doubt that he was *the* man for her. So Naomi told Ruth to bathe, put on perfume and wear the nicest of clothes and go visit Boaz. After Boaz had finished eating and drinking, Ruth visited him and laid at his feet. Ruth practically proposed to him and made herself sexually available to Boaz, yet he did the noble thing and didn't touch her. Boaz was a guardian-redeemer, which basically means he had the legal obligation to redeem a family member that was in serious difficulty.

Naomi's husband left their property in the care of someone else while they fled to Moab but once he and his sons died Naomi lost authority to manage or sell the property because she was a woman. If Boaz redeemed Ruth, he could then sell it or manage it along with his own property. But a problem occurred because there was another guardian-redeemer in closer relation than Boaz and he legally had the right to Ruth and her families' land before Boaz. Being a woman during this time was difficult. Ruth had little to no say about her life choices. Luckily, the other guy only wanted the land and not Ruth. So, Boaz redeemed the land and, in effect, took Ruth as his wife. Elimelek's poor move decision was then corrected through the faithfulness of Ruth and the family lineage was saved. The elders of Bethlehem compared the once Moabite woman to Rachel and Leah, matriarchs of Israel. God had given Ruth a great name among his people and had great plans through her and Boaz.

> *So Boaz took Ruth and she became his wife. When he made love to her, the Lord enabled her to conceive, and she gave birth to a son. The women said to Naomi: "Praise be to the Lord, who this day has not left you without a guardian-redeemer. May he become famous throughout Israel! He will renew your life and sustain you in your old age. For your daughter-in-law, who loves you and who is better to you than seven sons, has given him birth."*
>
> *Then Naomi took the child in her arms and cared for him. The women living there said, "Naomi has a son!" And they named him Obed. He was the father of Jesse, the father of David. Ruth 4:13-17 NIV*

And it's here that the lineage of Abraham was continued.

From Abraham to David: Abraham, Isaac, Jacob, Judah, Perez, Hezron, Ram, Amminadab, Nahshon, Salma, Boaz, Obed, Jesse, David.

SAUL

> *"Now here is the king you have chosen, the one you asked for; see, the Lord has set a king over you. If you fear the Lord and serve and obey him and do not rebel against his commands, and if both you and the king who reigns over you follow the Lord your God—good! But if you do not obey the Lord, and if you rebel against his commands, his hand will be against you, as it was against your ancestors." 1 Samuel 12:13-15 NIV*

Saul was the first king that God appointed over Israel. He was thirty years old when he became king and ruled over Israel for forty-two years.

He started off well, but the people wanted him for the wrong reasons. They wanted a king like the surrounding countries. He eventually became barbaric in his cruelty and his insecurity grew his rebellion against God.

> And the Lord regretted that he had made Saul king over Israel. 1 Samuel 15:35 NIV

DAVID

Then God appointed a man after his own heart as king!

> The Lord said to Samuel, "Fill your horn with oil and be on your way; I am sending you to Jesse of Bethlehem. I have chosen one of his sons to be king." 1 Samuel 16:1 NIV

After arriving in Bethlehem, Jesse brought seven of his sons before Samuel and one by one he declared the boys not chosen. But Jesse had one son that he didn't even consider bringing before Samuel—David, who was out tending sheep. *Go, find him and bring him back! For we will not even sit until he arrives.*

I can imagine everyone going every which way trying to find David out in the fields! And at once, they brought David before Samuel.

> Now he was ruddy and had beautiful eyes and was handsome. And the LORD said, "Arise, anoint him, for this is he!" 1 Samuel 16:12 ESV

Then Samuel anointed David as king with oil and God's Spirit rushed upon David from that day forward. But he still had some growing to do before God would place him on the throne.

CONQUERING GIANTS. Many times as humans, when we take on big tasks, giants seem to come our way. Obstacles seem to sit at our feet and hold on with full grip. It wasn't much different for David; except for his giant was Goliath—a giant among men. (Some say seven foot tall and others say nine. Either way, he was a beast of a man.) This story has ended up being one of the most famously told Bible story in Sunday school—which is ironic because it's gruesome.

David went out to battle.
He threw a stone at Goliath's head and killed him.
Then he walked up to the dude and cut off his head.

This is the story everyone wants to hear. We seek a hero! This is why superhero movies sell out every time! We love to watch the bad guy be brought to justice.

But, we have to remember that Saul was still king. David continued to do great things in Israel and he became a celebrity to the people. King Saul became jealous and tried to kill David many times but he escaped every time. But his jealousy only grew. His attempts became so fierce that David had to flee for his life and only returned once Saul was killed.

When David returned to Israel, the crown became his. But that didn't come without its own struggles. When Saul was killed, his army commander placed Saul's son, Ish-Bosheth, over Israel. He reigned for two years while David reigned over Judah. But his reign didn't last very long and he was killed. All the tribes of Israel came to David and anointed him as their king. No longer was David king just ruling Judah, but over all Israel. The future for the nation started to look good again with David on the throne.

A PLACE FOR THE LORD. First order of business you ask? A people called the Jebusites occupied the city of Jerusalem and David had better plans for it. So he conquered them and took their city, renaming it the City of David.

But that wasn't all!

This city was special. It was so special that he brought the Ark of Covenant there. Remember it? That's where the Ten Commandments are held and it sits within the Holy of Holies inside the Tabernacle.

David was so ecstatic that as the Ark was brought into the City of David he danced for joy! His heart incredibly overjoyed that the Ark would be near him again. He could do nothing else but celebrate before the Lord.

> *After David was settled in his palace, he said to Nathan the prophet, "Here I am, living in a house of cedar, while the ark of the covenant of the Lord is under a tent."*
>
> *Nathan replied to David, "Whatever you have in mind, do it, for God is with you."*
>
> *But that night the word of God came to Nathan, saying: "Go and tell my servant David, 'This is what the Lord says: You are not the one to build me a house to dwell in. I have not dwelt in a house from the day I brought Israel up out of Egypt to this day. I have moved from one tent site to another, from one dwelling place to another. Wherever I have*

moved with all the Israelites, did I ever say to any of their leaders whom I commanded to shepherd my people, "Why have you not built me a house of cedar?"'

"Now then, tell my servant David, 'This is what the Lord Almighty says: I took you from the pasture, from tending the flock, and appointed you ruler over my people Israel. I have been with you wherever you have gone, and I have cut off all your enemies from before you. Now I will make your name like the names of the greatest men on earth. And I will provide a place for my people Israel and will plant them so that they can have a home of their own and no longer be disturbed. Wicked people will not oppress them anymore, as they did at the beginning and have done ever since the time I appointed leaders over my people Israel. I will also subdue all your enemies.

I declare to you that the Lord will build a house for you: When your days are over and you go to be with your ancestors, I will raise up your offspring to succeed you, one of your own sons, and I will establish his kingdom. He is the one who will build a house for me, and I will establish his throne forever. I will be his father, and he will be my son. I will never take my love away from him, as I took it away from your predecessor. I will set him over my house and my kingdom forever; his throne will be established forever."

Nathan reported to David all the words of this entire revelation. 1 Chronicles 17:1-15 NIV

DAVID AND BATHSHEBA. By this point, David's reign was extremely successful. He did what was just and right among the people and conquered many surrounding nations in battle. But when things are going well . . . often times temptations come our way.

One evening David went up on his roof and saw a beautiful woman bathing across the way. He sent for her and brought her back to his room to sleep with her. A while later the woman, Bathsheba, sent word that she was pregnant. Her husband, one of David's soldiers, was off at war and she knew it wasn't his. Long story short, after trying to find an easy way to get out of the mess he'd made, he put Bathsheba's husband on the front line of the next battle and he was killed. David brought Bathsheba to his home as his wife and the whole matter greatly displeased the Lord.

God sent his prophet Nathan to speak some sense into David and rebuke him for his sin. David acknowledged the sin he had done and repented. And guess what? God forgave him! God forgives those who repent. David could do nothing else but sing to God.

Have mercy on me, O God,
according to your unfailing love;
according to your great compassion
blot out my transgressions.
Wash away all my iniquity
and cleanse me from my sin.
Create in me a pure heart, O God,
and renew a steadfast spirit within me.
Do not cast me from your presence
or take your Holy Spirit from me.
Restore to me the joy of your salvation
and grant me a willing spirit, to sustain me."
Psalm 51:1-2;10-12 NIV

DAVID'S FAREWELL. David's story ends with him purchasing a piece of property in Jerusalem from a Jebusite (remember, the people David conquered when he took over Jerusalem and moved in the Ark of Covenant? Those people!). And it's this same plot of land where David's son Solomon would soon build a temple for the Lord.

And so David, with all his money and power, could only sit, plan and wait for Solomon to do the building.

SOLOMON

A father's dream is that their son would walk in their footsteps. David's son Solomon took the throne in his father's old age and he was brilliant! He was best known for his wisdom and character. The book of 1 Kings tells of his reign, but he actually wrote three books: Proverbs, Ecclesiastes and Song of Solomon.

Four years after Solomon became king he began to build the temple of the Lord. The task that his father longed to do was in his grasp. It was massive and breath-taking. No longer would God reside in a portable tent, but now in a house.

In Solomon's reign, he continued to unify the people with one focus—to be one nation following one God. Did they always get it right? Definitely not! Tensions surrounded Israel towards the end of Solomon's life, but as long as he was alive unity remained.

THE DIVIDED KINGDOM

REHOBOAM. Solomon's son, Rehoboam, took over Kingship after Solomon's death and was a terrible ruler. His lack of leadership divided up the kingdom of Israel into two parts, Judah (South) and Israel (North).

KINGS

JEROBOAM. When the northern tribes lost confidence in Rehoboam they called for a new king.

> When all the Israelites heard that Jeroboam had returned, they sent and called him to the assembly and made him king over all Israel. Only the tribe of Judah remained loyal to the house of David. 1 Kings 12:20 NIV

Jeroboam began to lead the northern ten tribes of Israel but his leadership went to his head. He fell into the same trap that King Saul lost the throne to—jealousy. The Southern Kingdom had the temple but the Northern Kingdom didn't have anything connecting them to God.

Jereboam began to feel threatened by there only being one temple in Israel, and it was in the other kingdom's territory! *What if my people go offer sacrifices at the temple of the Lord in Jerusalem and pledge their allegiance again to the House of David?* Jeroboam wouldn't let this happen. So he had his men create two golden calves for the people to worship. *There's no need to go all the way to Jerusalem to make your sacrifices to God. Here are your gods who brought you out of Egypt! You will now bring your sacrifices here.*

ELIJAH AND ELISHA. Time and time again the kings led Israel astray and God sent prophets to call His people to repentance. God hated watching His children floundering in sin and showed them consequences for their disobedience.

Elijah was a mighty prophet. He prophesied during the reign of king Ahab who was a crude dude. His kingdom, much like the other kings who ruled over Israel, was corrupt. King Ahab and his people worshiped Baal and gave up on the Lord.

Elijah couldn't let this corruption go any longer and confronted King Ahab. Elijah knew the peoples allegiance to Baal and set up a duel between Baal and God. The four-hundred and fifty prophets of Baal took a bull and cut it into pieces and then placed it on an altar. Elijah challenged them to call out to Baal to set the sacrifice ablaze but no fire came. He began to taunt them, *Shout louder perhaps he is deep in thought or busy!* But no one answered. Elijah then rebuilt the altar of the Lord that had been torn down and placed his bull on the altar. He used twelve stones representing the twelve tribes of Israel—maybe this would remind the people of their prior allegiance to the one true God. He told the people to fill four large jars of water and pour it on the altar. Elijah prayed to the Lord to make Himself known to the people by showing His power. And in complete contrast to the silence of Baal, God revealed Himself by setting fire to the sacrifice! Not only did the fire consume the sacrifice it also burned up the wood, stones and soil as well. When the people saw God's power they could do nothing else but fall prostrate on the ground and cry out to God. He then killed every single prophet of Baal.

But King Ahab's allegiance wasn't swayed.

Ahab ran off to tell his wife Jezebel about everything Elijah had done. Jezebel was a ruthless queen when it came to getting her way. She was the daughter of the king of Tyre and wife of Israel's Northern King, Ahab (whom she had wrapped around her finger, by the way). Baal was her native god and no one was going to challenge her people to worship anything else. So she sent word to Elijah, *if I don't kill you may the gods kill me.* In other words, I won't give up until you are dead.

So Elijah fled for his life.

He cried out to the Lord to take his life and then fell asleep. When he woke up he found a jar of water and fresh baked bread over hot coals. The Lord was still present and taking care of His servant. The angel of the Lord touched Elijah and told him to get up and journey to Horeb, the Mountain of God.

> *God: "What are you doing here, Elijah?"*
>
> *Elijah: "I have been very zealous for the Lord God Almighty. The Israelites have rejected your covenant, torn down your altars, and put your prophets to death with the sword. I am the only one left, and now they are trying to kill me too."*
>
> *God: "Go out and stand on the mountain in the presence of the Lord, for the Lord is about to pass by."*
>
> *Then a great and powerful wind tore the mountains apart and shattered the rocks before the Lord, but the Lord was not in the wind. After the wind there was an earthquake, but the Lord was not in the earthquake. After the earthquake came a fire, but the Lord was not in the fire. And after the fire came a gentle whisper. When Elijah heard it, he pulled his cloak over his face and went out and stood at the mouth of the cave.*
>
> *God: "What are you doing here, Elijah?"*
>
> *Elijah: "I have been very zealous for the Lord God Almighty. The Israelites have rejected your covenant, torn down your altars, and put your prophets*

> *to death with the sword. I am the only one left, and now they are trying to kill me too." 1 Kings 19:9-14 NIV*

The repetition of the question, *what are you doing here* signifies that Elijah should be somewhere else. *Why are you in this cave when you ought to be my mouthpiece to the people?*

Nevertheless, God sent Elijah off on a new commission. First to anoint Hazael king over Aram (Israel's adversary) and Jehu king over Israel. And second, to anoint a man named Elisha as his successor. Both of which God sent Elijah back to the very place his spiritual journey took a detour.

He then did as the Lord God had commanded of him. Elijah prophesied through the reign of several kings. The spirituality of Israel was at stake between God and Baal throughout his entire ministry.

The time came for Elijah to be taken up to Heaven and Elisha took over Elijah's ministry for the Lord. Elisha did good in the eyes of the Lord and carried on the work of his predecessor. One of his greatest acts was killing Jezebel and King Ahab along with their family, ending their reign of injustice.

HOSHEA: THE LAST NORTHERN KING. King Hoshea did evil in the eyes of the Lord. Hoshea had an alliance with Shalmaneser, king of Assyria, but was disloyal. He decided to rebel against the king and so he invaded the Northern Kingdom of Israel and seized the land.

Assyria took Israelites captive and placed their own people in Samaria; God sent lions to devour them and the King of Assyria ordered priests who were exiled to go back and teach the people what the Lord requires so they could live. But the people then made their own shrines and worshiped what they wanted. So they worshiped both God and gods.

JOSIAH. Time after time, the rulers over Israel led the people astray. The Northern Kingdom didn't have one single good ruler after Jeroboam tore the kingdom apart. But, the Southern Kingdom had a few good guys like Asa, Jehoshaphat, Hezekiah and Josiah.

The overall nation of Israel was in despair. The North had lost their way entirely and the South wasn't very far behind them. The Southern Kingdom had a rough set of consecutive kings and the nation set God almost completely on the backburner. Idolatry was the new norm.

Can you imagine?
Let's take a step back.

The entire world was worshiping idols and living unholy lives. So God called one nation, Israel, to be an example for the rest of world to follow . . . and that entire nation had fallen away from God?

Yes.

But, God raised up a king whose name was Josiah. He was eight years old when his father's throne was passed onto him. Can you imagine an eight-year-old running a nation?

(My son is several weeks away from being born and to think in eight years he would reign over a nation would be far from believable. Yet, Josiah led his kingdom to follow God! Keep reading on.)

Josiah led the people very well. But God was still not the focal point of the nation. One day while the temple was being repaired. The high priest found the Book of the Law and immediately brought it before the king.

> When the king heard the words of the Book of the Law, he tore his robes. He gave these orders to Hilkiah the priest, Ahikam son of Shaphan, Akbor son of Micaiah, Shaphan the secretary and Asaiah the king's attendant: "Go and inquire of the Lord for me and for the people and for all Judah about what is written in this book that has been found. Great is the Lord's anger that burns against us because those who have gone before us have not obeyed the words of this book; they have not acted in accordance with all that is written there concerning us." 2 Kings 22:11-13 NIV

The Lord brought word to Josiah of His anger that burned against Israel for abandoning Him.

Can you sense God's pain?

It was then that Josiah renewed the Southern Kingdom's covenant with God. He tore down all the idols that the previous kings had erected and placed the Book of the Law as the ruling authority over Israel. His goal was for the people of Israel to follow God once again.

After Josiah's death, the following southern kings were corrupt and didn't follow in Josiah's footsteps.

PROPHETS

CHAPTER TWELVE

Children have I reared and brought up, but they have rebelled against me. Isaiah 1:2 ESV

PRE-EXILE: REBELLION

The nation of Israel became so corrupt that God sent prophets to spur the people back into a Godly nation. As you've read in the previous chapter, many of Israel's kings led the people away from the one true God. Over and over again, God called His people back to Him yet they continually ran the other way to worship other gods. You'll see soon that their rebellion led them to their ultimate consequence.

JONAH. *The word of the Lord came to Jonah: "Go to the great city of Nineveh and preach against it, because its wickedness has come up before me." But Jonah ran away from the Lord and headed for Tarshish. Jonah 1:1-3 NIV*

(Side Note: It was a 2,500-mile journey to Tarshish [Spain] instead of the 550-mile journey to Nineveh [Iraq].)

Jonah then paid a fare to board a ship in Joppa to head for Tarshish. He wanted to get as far away from the Assyrians as he could get, but he couldn't flee from God.

God sent a great storm to get Jonah's attention and the boat looked like it was going to be destroyed. The sailors were scared and each cried out to their own gods but nothing changed. The storm was still fierce. They went below deck to grab cargo to throw overboard in hope to lighten their load and there they found Jonah, fast asleep. *Wake up! Call your god... maybe he can save us!* The sailors cast lots and the lot fell on Jonah so they asked him, *what did you do to cause this much trouble? Who is responsible for this storm?* Jonah knew it was his fault and that God was punishing him. So he told the men about his God and how He is the God of the sea and the land. The sailors asked, *what should we do to calm the seas?* Jonah told the men to throw him overboard and then the seas would calm. After some convincing they threw him overboard and the storm ceased. The men could do nothing else but worship God.

God sent a huge fish to swallow Jonah and he stayed in its belly for three days and three nights! Can you imagine being alive and surrounded by the junk the fish had swallowed? This was not a cruise line I would like to try!

From the belly of the fish Jonah began to pray.

> *"In my distress I called to the Lord, and he answered me. From deep in the realm of the dead I called for help, and you listened to my cry. You hurled me into the depths, into the very heart of*

the seas, and the currents swirled about me; all your waves and breakers swept over me. I said, 'I have been banished from your sight; yet I will look again toward your holy temple.' The engulfing waters threatened me, the deep surrounded me; seaweed was wrapped around my head. To the roots of the mountains I sank down; the earth beneath barred me in forever. But you, Lord my God, brought my life up from the pit. When my life was ebbing away, I remembered you, Lord, and my prayer rose to you, to your holy temple. Those who cling to worthless idols turn away from God's love for them. But I, with shouts of grateful praise, will sacrifice to you. What I have vowed I will make good. I will say, 'Salvation comes from the Lord.'"

And the Lord commanded the fish, and it vomited Jonah onto dry land. Jonah 2:1-10 NIV

God then came to Jonah a second time and called him to preach to Nineveh. This time Jonah went.

(Side note: Nineveh means "House of the fish" and they worshiped a fish god. God sent Jonah to preach to the city that worshiped a fish. When Jonah didn't listen, God sent a great fish to swallow Jonah and take him there. Yeah, God is witty.)

Jonah's message wasn't very encouraging. He went into this large city and began to shout, *forty days or you shall be overthrown!* Basically, turn from your evil ways or burn. And guess what happened next! The people of Nineveh repented to God of their sins. Their king ordered everyone and their animals to fast and put on funeral clothes to mourn for their sinful ways. God saw how they turned from their evil ways and changed His mind about bringing judgment upon them.

Jonah hated Nineveh and burned with anger for the mercy God gave them. Nineveh was a powerful city and was the capitol of Assyria. Nineveh was cruel and barbaric and Jonah didn't want anything to do with them. Israel was God's chosen people and that was enough for Jonah. But for God, these people were just as much His creation as Israel was. Israel was God's chosen people to be an example to the world; though Israel failed in this time and time again. Of course God would save Nineveh, they were His children. Israel was God's "chosen people" but they were not His only people.

Jonah is a fitting prophet to start off this chapter because he greatly represents where Israel was spiritually during his ministry. Israel felt entitled to do what they wanted and didn't want to listen to God.

JOEL. Joel prophesied to the Southern Kingdom of Judah. He began his speech with imagery of a locust plague devouring vegetation in Israel. What we might read as random was incredibly important to Israel. Their main source of income was olive oil, wine, and grain. Israel as a whole was turning away from God at a rapid speed. Yet they were holding on to God's precious gifts to them – vegetation. This gave them an income and it also allowed for them to sit back and indulge in drinking wine. They allowed these luxuries to pull them away from their worship. These things alone were not bad. But Israel gave them too much of their attention and gave God next to none. Joel gave warning that their priorities needed to change and if they didn't . . . a plague was on its way. But instead of locusts, it would be another country's army.

"Wake up, you drunkards, and weep! Wail, all you drinkers of wine; wail because of the new wine, for

> it has been snatched from your lips. A nation has invaded my land, a mighty army without number; it has the teeth of a lion, the fangs of a lioness. It has laid waste my vines and ruined my fig trees. It has stripped off their bark and thrown it away, leaving their branches white.
>
> Let all who live in the land tremble, for the day of the Lord is coming. It is close at hand—a day of darkness and gloom, a day of clouds and blackness. Like dawn spreading across the mountains a large and mighty army comes, such as never was in ancient times nor ever will be in ages to come." Joel 1:5-7; 2:1-2 NIV

> "Even now," declares the Lord, "return to me with all your heart, with fasting and weeping and mourning. Rend your heart and not your garments. Return to the Lord your God, for he is gracious and compassionate, slow to anger and abounding in love, and he relents from sending calamity" Joel 2:12-13 NIV

God's love is tremendously better than that between a father and his children. In parenting, we shouldn't enjoy giving consequences for our children's bad actions, but we do it to help them make better decisions in the future. God sent word to His children that if they continued to pursue evil, they would gain a consequence. But if they repented and followed Him, then they would be forgiven.

> Then the Lord was jealous for his land and took pity on his people. The Lord replied to them: "I am sending you grain, new wine and olive oil, enough to satisfy you fully; never again will I make you an object of scorn to the nations. I will drive the northern horde far from you, pushing it into a parched and barren land." Joel 2:18-20 NIV

> "Then you will know that I, the Lord your God, dwell in Zion, my holy hill. Jerusalem will be holy; never again will foreigners invade her." Joel 3:17 NIV

AMOS. God sent Amos to speak to the Northern Kingdom of Israel. They still worshiped God but their hearts weren't fully in it. They were definitely worse off than the Southern Kingdom at that point. They were too consumed with their self-righteous sin that they lost sight of God and their calling as a nation. They were called to be an example to the world, but they looked more like the world than like God.

Amos first spoke judgments about Israel's surrounding nations and then on Judah before moving on to the Northern Kingdom of Israel. God doesn't play favorites. Sin is sin. Israel's two kingdoms were still split since the death of Solomon and the wounds had yet to heal.

Israel continued to rebel and their impending consequence was knocking at their door. There would soon be a time where their evil deeds would catch up to them and Assyria would invade Israel and take their land. But God prophesied through Amos of a time of restoration.

> "In that day I will restore David's fallen shelter—I will repair its broken walls and restore its ruins—and will rebuild it as it used to be." Amos 9:11 NIV

HOSEA. God called Hosea to do something radical and scandalous. Typically, a prophet was called up to go speak to a people on behalf of God. But Hosea was called to love a promiscuous woman illustrating God's love for Israel.

> When the Lord began to speak through Hosea, the Lord said to him, "Go, marry a promiscuous wom-

> an and have children with her, for like an adulterous wife this land is guilty of unfaithfulness to the Lord." Hosea 1:2 NIV

So Hosea went and married a woman named Gomer. I imagine Hosea racing to the store to buy everything he needed to decorate the house to have it ready for her arrival.

Hosea pursued Gomer.
After they were married, Gomer became pregnant and gave birth to a son giving him the name Jezreel. His name was a literal reminder of God's disapproval of bloodshed by a former king in the town of Jezreel. Basically, Israel . . . you're not acting the way you've been called to act. You're unjust!

> Gomer conceived again and gave birth to a daughter. Then the Lord said to Hosea, "Call her Lo-Ruhamah (which means "not loved"), for I will no longer show love to Israel, that I should at all forgive them. Yet I will show love to Judah; and I will save them." Hosea 1:6-7 NIV

Then Gomer conceived another son and God named him

> "Lo-Ammi (which means "not my people"), for you are not my people, and I am not your God." Hosea 1:8 NIV

Gomer came from a dangerous lifestyle. But, it was her "normal". The lifestyle she walked into with Hosea was new. We don't know the exact details, but we do know Gomer left Hosea. Maybe having a husband who truly cared for her became too much. She wasn't used to real affection.

> The Lord said to Hosea, "Go, show your love to your wife again, though she is loved by another man and is an adulteress. Love her as the Lord loves the Israelites, though they turn to other gods."
>
> So Hosea bought her for fifteen shekels of silver and about a homer and a lethek of barley. Hosea 3:1-2 NIV

This is the story of God and Israel. Israel continued to run away from God's love. God knew if they ran away from HHHis direction they would be in trouble. We have rules to keep us from getting hurt but this was the situation Israel kept finding itself in. God's love was the real deal but they had become numb to real love and ran the other way.

But God was going to buy them back.

> "Hear the word of the Lord, you Israelites, because the Lord has a charge to bring against you who live in the land: 'There is no faithfulness, no love, no acknowledgment of God in the land. There is only cursing, lying and murder, stealing and adultery; they break all bounds, and bloodshed follows bloodshed. A spirit of prostitution leads them astray; they are unfaithful to their God.'" Hosea 4:1-3, 12 NIV
>
> "My God will reject them because they have not obeyed him; they will be wanderers among the nations." Hosea 9:17 NIV
>
> "When Israel was a child, I loved him, and out of Egypt I called my son. But the more they were called, the more they went away from me. They

> sacrificed to the [gods of] Baal and they burned incense to images." Hosea 11:1-2 NIV

Hosea was in a tough position. God was fed up with Israel abandoning Him and disregarding His loving gestures. Hosea called the Israelites to return to the Lord, but they continued to prostitute themselves to other gods.

ISAIAH. *The vision of Isaiah . . . which he saw concerning Judah and Jerusalem.*

> "Hear, O heavens, and give ear, O earth; for the Lord has spoken: 'Children have I reared and brought up, but they have rebelled against me.'
>
> Ah, sinful nation, a people laden with iniquity, they have forsaken the Lord, they have despised the Holy One of Israel, they are utterly estranged. Why will you still be struck down? Why will you continue to rebel?" Isaiah 1:1-5 ESV

Israel needed someone to save them from their brokenness. Time after time the prophets spoke but the people didn't listen. They needed someone greater. They needed a Savior. Isaiah envisions a time when that Savior is born.

> "For to us a child is born, to us a son is given, and the government will be on his shoulders. And he will be called Wonderful Counselor, Mighty God, Everlasting Father, Prince of Peace. Of the greatness of his government and peace there will be no end. He will reign on David's throne and over his kingdom, establishing and upholding it with justice and righteousness from that time on and forever." Isaiah 9:6 NIV

But in the meantime, more prophets were on their way.

MICAH. Micah's audience was Judah. The divided kingdom of Israel was dwindling in power and justice. God's people needed to be redirected but they continued to fall away.

> "Hear, you peoples, all of you, listen, earth and all who live in it, that the Sovereign Lord may bear witness against you, the Lord from his holy temple." Micah 1:2 NIV

> "Woe to those who plan iniquity, to those who plot evil on their beds! At morning's light they carry it out because it is in their power to do it. They covet fields and seize them, and houses, and take them. They defraud people of their homes; they rob them of their inheritance. Therefore, the Lord says: 'I am planning disaster against this people, from which you cannot save yourselves. You will no longer walk proudly, for it will be a time of calamity'". Micah 2:1-3 NIV

> "Get up, go away! For this is not your resting place, because it is defiled, it is ruined, beyond all remedy." Micah 2:10 NIV

> "In the last days the mountain of the Lord's temple will be established as the highest of the mountains; it will be exalted above the hills, and peoples will stream to it. Many nations will come and say, 'Come, let us go up to the mountain of the Lord, to the temple of the God of Jacob. He will teach us his ways, so that we may walk in his paths.'
>
> In that day, declares the Lord, I will gather the lame; I will assemble the exiles and those I have brought to grief. I will make the lame my remnant, those driven away a strong nation. The Lord will rule over them in Mount Zion from that day and forever." Micah 4:1-2, 6-7 NIV

PROPHETS

And again we see the sign of a Savior to be born.

> *"Bethlehem, though you are small among the clans of Judah, out of you will come for me one who will be ruler over Israel, whose origins are from of old, from ancient times." Micah 5:2 NIV*

NAHUM. The prophet Jonah (after much prompting by God) preached to Nineveh. It was one of the greatest revivals in all history. Nineveh turned from their sin and worshiped God. But years later they stirred up trouble again. They plotted evil against Israel and God had had enough of it.

> *"The Lord is a jealous and avenging God; the Lord takes vengeance and is filled with wrath. The Lord takes vengeance on his foes and vents his wrath against his enemies. The Lord is slow to anger but great in power; the Lord will not leave the guilty unpunished." Nahum 1:2-3 NIV*

> *"The Lord is good, a refuge in times of trouble. He cares for those who trust in him, but with an overwhelming flood he will make an end of Nineveh; he will pursue his foes into the realm of darkness. Whatever they plot against the Lord he will bring to an end." Nahum 1:7-9 NIV*

> *"King of Assyria, your shepherds slumber; your nobles lie down to rest. Your people are scattered on the mountains with no one to gather them. Nothing can heal you; your wound is fatal. All who hear the news about you clap their hands at your fall, for who has not felt your endless cruelty?" Nahum 3:18-19 NIV*

ZEPHANIAH. *"I will sweep away everything from the face of the earth," declares the Lord. "I will sweep away both man and beast; I will sweep away the birds in*

> the sky and the fish in the sea—and the idols that cause the wicked to stumble." "When I destroy all mankind on the face of the earth," declares the Lord, "I will stretch out my hand against Judah and against all who live in Jerusalem. I will destroy every remnant of Baal worship in this place. Be silent before the Sovereign Lord, for the day of the Lord is near." Zephaniah 1:2-4, 7 NIV

First, God spoke judgment on Judah.

> *"Gather together, gather yourselves together, you shameful nation, before the decree takes effect and that day passes like windblown chaff, before the Lord's fierce anger comes upon you, before the day of the Lord's wrath comes upon you. Seek the Lord, all you humble of the land, you who do what he commands. Seek righteousness, seek humility; perhaps you will be sheltered on the day of the Lord's anger." Zephaniah 2:1-3 NIV*

But God didn't stop there. He then spoke judgment on surrounding nations: Philistia, Moab, Ammon, Cush and Assyria.

And then God turned to the city of Jerusalem, the city that was supposed to be the religious hub of the nation.

> *"Woe to the city of oppressors, rebellious and defiled! She obeys no one, she accepts no correction. She does not trust in the Lord, she does not draw near to her God. Her officials within her are roaring lions; her rulers are evening wolves, who leave nothing for the morning. Her prophets are unprincipled; they are treacherous people. Her priests profane the sanctuary and do violence to the law. The Lord within her is righteous; he does no wrong. Morning by morning he dispenses his jus-*

> tice, and every new day he does not fail, yet the unrighteous know no shame.
>
> Jerusalem I thought, 'Surely you will fear me and accept correction!' Then her place of refuge would not be destroyed, nor all my punishments come upon her. But they were still eager to act corruptly in all they did. Therefore wait for me," declares the Lord, "for the day I will stand up to testify. I have decided to assemble the nations, to gather the kingdoms and to pour out my wrath on them—all my fierce anger. The whole world will be consumed by the fire of my jealous anger. Then I will purify the lips of the peoples, that all of them may call on the name of the Lord and serve him shoulder to shoulder." Zephaniah 3:1-5, 7-9 NIV

Zephaniah ends his book with a vision of restoration for Israel. God would redeem His remnant and purify their lips so they would no longer call to lifeless idols but call on the name of the Lord.

HABAKKUK. At this point in Israel's history the nation had become so unjust that a prophet named Habakkuk had to do something about it. Instead of him addressing the people, he addressed God.

> *Habakkuk:* "How long, Lord, must I call for help, but you do not listen? Or cry out to you, 'Violence!' but you do not save? Why do you make me look at injustice? Why do you tolerate wrongdoing?" Habakkuk 1:2-3 NIV

But of course God had a response. Habakkuk thought God was just sitting around, but He was already at work.

> *God:* "Look at the nations and watch—and be utterly amazed. For I am going to do something

> *in your days that you would not believe, even if you were told. I am raising up the Babylonians, that ruthless and impetuous people, who sweep across the whole earth to seize dwellings not their own." Habakkuk 1:5-6 NIV*

> *Habakkuk: "Lord, are you not from everlasting? My God, my Holy One, you will never die. You, Lord, have appointed them to execute judgment; you, my Rock, have ordained them to punish. Your eyes are too pure to look on evil; you cannot tolerate wrongdoing. Why then do you tolerate the treacherous? Why are you silent while the wicked swallow up those more righteous than themselves?" Habakkuk 1:12-13 NIV*

God acknowledged Habakkuk's anger about His course of action. But He also reminded him of Israel's cruel injustice that Habakkuk brought before Him. *They have stolen! They have plundered many nations! They have murdered! They have taken advantage of others! They have become drunks. They worship lifeless gods!* In hearing God's words he began to understand the Father's consequence for His children.

> *Habakkuk: "Lord, I have heard of your fame; I stand in awe of your deeds, Lord. Repeat them in our day, in our time make them known; in wrath remember mercy." Habakkuk 3:2 NIV*

JEREMIAH. He spoke to Judah in the last days before Babylon destroyed Israel.

> *God: "Before I formed you in the womb I knew you, before you were born I set you apart; I appointed you as a prophet to the nations."*

PROPHETS

Jeremiah: "Alas, Sovereign Lord, I do not know how to speak; I am too young."

God: "Do not say, 'I am too young.' You must go to everyone I send you to and say whatever I command you. Do not be afraid of them, for I am with you and will rescue you."

God reached out His hand and touched Jeremiah's mouth and said to him:

God: "I have put my words in your mouth. See, today I appoint you over nations and kingdoms to uproot and tear down, to destroy and overthrow, to build and to plant." Jeremiah 1:4-10 NIV

"From the north disaster will be poured out on all who live in the land. I am about to summon all the peoples of the northern kingdoms. Their kings will come and set up their thrones in the entrance of the gates of Jerusalem; they will come against all her surrounding walls and against all the towns of Judah. I will pronounce my judgments on my people because of their wickedness in forsaking me, in burning incense to other gods and in worshiping what their hands have made. Get yourself ready! Stand up and say to them whatever I command you. Do not be terrified by them, or I will terrify you before them." Jeremiah 1:14-17 NIV

"Yet even in those days, I will not destroy you completely. And when the people ask, 'Why has the Lord our God done all this to us?' you will tell them, 'As you have forsaken me and served foreign gods in your own land, so now you will serve foreigners in a land not your own.'" Jeremiah 5:18-19 NIV

God was fed up with Israel's attitude toward Him. As a father looking to His children, God was hurt by the

covenant Israel was breaking. When God brought the Israelites out of Egypt, He made a covenant with them. Follow me and obey my commandments and you will be my children and I will be your father. Then I will gift you a land that possesses all you'll ever need. You will be my people and I will be your God. Israel had lost connection to God and crushed the covenant between them. The land was a gift of their covenant. But now it was time for the gift to be taken away.

> *"Gather up your belongings to leave the land, you who live under siege. For this is what the Lord says: 'At this time I will hurl out those who live in this land; I will bring distress on them so that they may be captured.'" Jeremiah 10:17-18 NIV*

The crime: Decades of spiritual prostitution and injustice. The penalty: Seventy years of exile. Many of the prophets foretold of a time when restoration would be brought upon Israel, yet they didn't get to see it for themselves.

> *This is what the Lord Almighty, the God of Israel, says to all those I carried into exile from Jerusalem to Babylon: "Build houses and settle down; plant gardens and eat what they produce. Marry and have sons and daughters; find wives for your sons and give your daughters in marriage, so that they too may have sons and daughters. Increase in number there; do not decrease. Also, seek the peace and prosperity of the city to which I have carried you into exile. Pray to the Lord for it, because if it prospers, you too will prosper."*

> *This is what the Lord says: "When seventy years are completed for Babylon, I will come to you and fulfill my good promise to bring you back to this place. For I know the plans I have for you," declares the Lord, "plans to prosper you and not to harm you,*

plans to give you hope and a future. Then you will call on me and come and pray to me, and I will listen to you. You will seek me and find me when you seek me with all your heart. I will be found by you," declares the Lord. Jeremiah 29:4-7, 10-14 NIV

EXILE: THE FALL OF ISRAEL

Then God's people went into exile. They became refugees in a foreign land. The major messages of the prophets were that the people were so wicked and idolatrous that exile was inevitable. Their only hope was God's promise that He would redeem them and bring them back to the land God had gifted them.

EZEKIEL. Ezekiel spoke to the exiles in Babylon giving them hope of a future restoration of Israel. God would cleanse His people and rebuild His temple. Israel would be made holy again.

> *"It is not for your sake, people of Israel, that I am going to do these things, but for the sake of my holy name, which you have profaned among the nations where you have gone. I will show the holiness of my great name, which has been profaned among the nations, the name you have profaned among them. Then the nations will know that I am the Lord, declares the Sovereign Lord, when I am proved holy through you before their eyes.*
>
> *For I will take you out of the nations; I will gather you from all the countries and bring you back into your own land. I will sprinkle clean water on you, and you will be clean; I will cleanse you from all your impurities and from all your idols. I will give you a new heart and put a new spirit in you; I will remove from you your heart of stone and give you a heart of flesh. And I will put my Spirit in you and*

> *move you to follow my decrees and be careful to keep my laws. Then you will live in the land I gave your ancestors; you will be my people, and I will be your God. I will save you from all your uncleanness." Ezekiel 36:22-29 NIV*

OBADIAH. During the exile of Israel, Edom saw an opportunity to invade and steal from the land. This greatly angered God.

> *"The day of the Lord is near for all nations. As you have done, it will be done to you; your deeds will return upon your own head. Just as you drank on my holy hill, so all the nations will drink continually; they will drink and drink and be as if they had never been. But on Mount Zion will be deliverance; it will be holy, and Jacob will possess his inheritance. Jacob will be a fire and Joseph a flame; Esau will be stubble, and they will set him on fire and destroy him. There will be no survivors from Esau." The Lord has spoken. Obadiah 1:15-18 NIV*

(Side note: Edomites are the descendants of Esau and Israel the descendants of Jacob. Jacob's name changed to Israel when God blessed him. These twins fought in the womb and still to this day have not found peace as nations.)

DANIEL. Daniel was taken captive to Babylon at a young age. He then rose to power in Babylon as their Prime Minister. Babylon was at his throat, but he continued to live in obedience to God. God blessed him with wisdom and the ability to interpret dreams. He also prophesied about the future.

> *In the third year of the reign of Jehoiakim king of Judah, Nebuchadnezzar king of Babylon came to*

Jerusalem and besieged it. And the Lord delivered Jehoiakim king of Judah into his hand, along with some of the articles from the temple of God. These he carried off to the temple of his god in Babylon and put in the treasure house of his god.

Then the king ordered Ashpenaz, chief of his court officials, to bring into the king's service some of the Israelites from the royal family and the nobility— young men without any physical defect, handsome, showing aptitude for every kind of learning, well informed, quick to understand, and qualified to serve in the king's palace. He was to teach them the language and literature of the Babylonians. The king assigned them a daily amount of food and wine from the king's table. They were to be trained for three years, and after that they were to enter the king's service. Among those who were chosen were some from Judah: Daniel, Hananiah, Mishael and Azariah. The chief official gave them new names: to Daniel, the name Belteshazzar; to Hananiah, Shadrach; to Mishael, Meshach; and to Azariah, Abednego. Daniel 1:1-7 NIV

The king's royal service to the men was well received, but Daniel could not imagine defiling himself with the non-kosher foods. God caused the chief official to show favor on the men but he was afraid to not follow through with the orders King Nebuchadnezzar had given him. *What if by not eating this food you become weak and frail? What then will the king say to me?* Daniel told the official to test him and the other men for ten days with eating only vegetables and drinking only water then comparing their appearance to the other men. At the end of the ten days they looked healthier and better nourished than the other men who ate the royal food.

To these four young men God gave knowledge and understanding of all kinds of literature and

> *learning. And Daniel could understand visions and dreams of all kinds.*
>
> *At the end of the time set by the king to bring them into his service, the chief official presented them to Nebuchadnezzar. The king talked with them, and he found none equal to Daniel, Hananiah, Mishael and Azariah; so they entered the king's service. In every matter of wisdom and understanding about which the king questioned them, he found them ten times better than all the magicians and enchanters in his whole kingdom. And Daniel remained there until the first year of King Cyrus. Daniel 1:17-21 NIV*

Following in Joseph's footsteps, God gifted Daniel the ability to interpret dreams. It was through this gift that King Nebuchadnezzar saw the glory of God and placed Daniel ruler over the province of Babylon. And beside him were Shadrach, Meshach and Abednego as his administrators.

Even in the midst of turmoil and exile God's placed His people in leadership.

But the story doesn't end there for these men. The king was fascinated with Daniel, Shadrach, Meshach and Abednego, but that didn't mean that he set his standards aside. Nebuchadnezzar, and his son who became king after him, had expectations of their people to worship them.

For the Babylonians this was normal. Kings in these days were worshiped as gods. But for God's righteous men this was not an option. Shadrach, Meshach and Abednego were caught not bowing before a 90-foot statue of the king and Daniel was seen praying to God while worship in Babylon was reserved only to the king. Both instances didn't come without punishment. A pit full of lions for Daniel and a fiery furnace for the other three. But death could not hold these men. God saved them from their punishment in their dedication to Him and made the king see His glory.

In Daniel's mourning he cried out to the Lord in prayer.

> *"Lord, the great and awesome God, who keeps his covenant of love with those who love him and keep his commandments, we have sinned and done wrong. We have been wicked and have rebelled; we have turned away from your commands and laws. We have not listened to your servants the prophets, who spoke in your name to our kings, our princes and our ancestors, and to all the people of the land. Lord, you are righteous, but this day we are covered with shame—the people of Judah and the inhabitants of Jerusalem and all Israel, both near and far, in all the countries where you have scattered us because of our unfaithfulness to you." Daniel 9:4-7 NIV*

POST-EXILE: RELEASE AND REBUILD

After seventy years, Israel's sentence was complete and they were to return to their land. But there were rules. The people needed to obey God's commands and rebuild. Their previous behavior would not be accepted. They were to be a holy nation.

EZRA. *"In the first year of Cyrus king of Persia, in order to fulfill the word of the Lord spoken by Jeremiah, the Lord moved the heart of Cyrus king of Persia to make a proclamation throughout his realm and also to put it in writing: This is what Cyrus king of Persia says: 'The Lord, the God of heaven, has*

> given me all the kingdoms of the earth and he has appointed me to build a temple for him at Jerusalem in Judah. Any of his people among you may go up to Jerusalem in Judah and build the temple of the Lord, the God of Israel, the God who is in Jerusalem, and may their God be with them. And in any locality where survivors may now be living, the people are to provide them with silver and gold, with goods and livestock, and with freewill offerings for the temple of God in Jerusalem.'" Ezra 1:1-4 NIV

HAGGAI. With King Cyrus' decree, many of the Jews returned to Israel. He paid the expense for the new temple. Once Israel returned they were excited to rebuild the temple. But, in time they became more focused on building their own homes. Haggai reminded them to put God first.

> This is what the Lord Almighty says: "These people say, 'The time has not yet come to rebuild the Lord's house.' Is it a time for you yourselves to be living in your paneled houses, while this house remains a ruin?" Haggai 1:2-4 NIV

> "Who of you is left who saw this house in its former glory? How does it look to you now? Does it not seem to you like nothing? But now be strong, Zerubbabel," declares the Lord. "Be strong, Joshua son of Jozadak, the high priest. Be strong, all you people of the land," declares the Lord, "and work. For I am with you," declares the Lord Almghty. "This is what I covenanted with you when you came out of Egypt. And my Spirit remains among you. Do not fear." Haggai 2:3-5 NIV

ESTHER. While many Jews had returned to Israel, some were left scattered in Persia. An Israelite girl named

Esther was born in Susa; the capitol of Persia. When she grew of age, King Ahasuerus (or possibly better known as Xerxes from the Battle of 300) found her beautiful and married her.

Haman, one of the king's officials, hated the Jews and created an ordinance to have them killed. But when Esther found out his plan she hurt for her people and fell at the feet of the king begging him to stop Haman's plan.

> *Esther:* *"If it pleases the king," she said, "and if he regards me with favor and thinks it the right thing to do, and if he is pleased with me, let an order be written overruling the dispatches that Haman devised and wrote to destroy the Jews in all the king's provinces. For how can I bear to see disaster fall on my people? How can I bear to see the destruction of my family?"*
>
> *King Xerxes:* *"Because Haman attacked the Jews, I have given his estate to Esther, and they have impaled him on the pole he set up. Now write another decree in the king's name in behalf of the Jews as seems best to you, and seal it with the king's signet ring—for no document written in the king's name and sealed with his ring can be revoked."* Esther 8:5-8 NIV

Esther then proceeded to write an ordinance to release the Jews. Haman's plan was over and God's people were free!

ZECHARIAH. Zechariah prophesied to Israel in preparation to rebuild the nation. Once again Israel will be a holy nation and out of it will come a king who redeems us all.

> *"The Lord was very angry with your ancestors. Therefore tell the people: This is what the Lord Al-*

> *mighty says: 'Return to me and I will return to you.' Do not be like your ancestors, to whom the earlier prophets proclaimed: This is what the Lord Almighty says: 'Turn from your evil ways and your evil practices.' But they would not listen or pay attention to me. Where are your ancestors now? And the prophets, do they live forever? But did not my words and my decrees, which I commanded my servants the prophets, overtake your ancestors? Then they repented and said, 'The Lord Almighty has done to us what our ways and practices deserve, just as he determined to do.'*
>
> *I am very jealous for Zion; I am burning with jealousy for her. I will return to Zion and dwell in Jerusalem. Then Jerusalem will be called the Faithful City, and the mountain of the Lord Almighty will be called the Holy Mountain. Once again men and women of ripe old age will sit in the streets of Jerusalem, each of them with cane in hand because of their age. The city streets will be filled with boys and girls playing there."* Zechariah 1:2-6; 8:2-5 NIV

In God's great excitement for the return of His children, He prophesied of the greatest king of all; His son, Christ, who would take away the sins of the world!

> *"Rejoice greatly, Daughter Zion! Shout, Daughter Jerusalem!*
>
> *See, your king comes to you, righteous and victorious, lowly and riding on a donkey, on a colt, the foal of a donkey. I will take away the chariots from Ephraim and the warhorses from Jerusalem, and the battle bow will be broken. He will proclaim peace to the nations. His rule will extend from sea to sea and from the River to the ends of the earth."* Zechariah 9:9-10 NIV

NEHEMIAH and EZRA. Nehemiah returned from exile after the temple had been built. He became the Governor of Jerusalem and built a protective wall around the city. The wall was completed in fifty-two days!

> When all our enemies heard about this, all the surrounding nations were afraid and lost their self-confidence, because they realized that this work had been done with the help of our God. Nehemiah 6:16 NIV

Imagine the destruction the exile brought on Israel. The temple was in shambles and raiders demolished the homes.

Now, it had been seven months after the people were back in their own land and Ezra, their priest, picked up an old dusty Bible and read it aloud to the people. The people had been in exile so it was probably the first time for many of the people to hear God's Word. And for others it had probably been a while.

> Ezra the priest brought the Law before the assembly, which was made up of men and women and all who were able to understand. He read it aloud from daybreak till noon as he faced the square before the Water Gate in the presence of the men, women and others who could understand. And all the people listened attentively to the Book of the Law. Nehemiah 8:2-3 NIV

After the reading of the Law of Moses, the people began to reflect on their own lives. They mourned for their sin and confessed them to God. Israel was turning a corner and finally putting their focus on God.

> *All who separated themselves from the neighboring peoples for the sake of the Law of God, together with their wives and all their sons and daughters who are able to understand—all these now join their fellow Israelites the nobles, and bind themselves with a curse and an oath to follow the Law of God given through Moses the servant of God and to obey carefully all the commands, regulations and decrees of the Lord our Lord. Nehemiah 10:28-29 NIV*

MALACHI. But sadly, Israel fell back into their sinful ways and God needed to revive them. They were lazy with their worship and unjust in their actions. God sent one last prophet to stir the hearts of Israel to renew their commitment to the Lord.

> *"Surely the day [of the Lord] is coming; it will burn like a furnace. But for you who revere my name, the sun of righteousness will rise with healing in its rays. Remember the law of my servant Moses, the decrees and laws I gave him at Horeb for all Israel." Malachi 4:1-2, 4 NIV*

God ends Malachi's book, and better yet the Old Testament as a whole, with an urge to cling to His word and to live by it. For those who do will find righteousness but those who do not will find judgment.

Now, to the One who saves us all!

PART FIVE
The New Testament

JESUS

CHAPTER THIRTEEN

Behold, the virgin shall conceive and bear a son, and they shall call his name Immanuel Matthew 1:23 ESV

WITHIN THE SILENCE

The Biblical silence between the Old and New Testaments are ironically not so silent. To better understand the opening pages of the first four books of the New Testament, known as the Gospels, you'll want to know what happened between Malachi and Matthew.

In the final books of the Old Testament we see the fall of Israel and the rise of three foreign super powers: Assyria, Babylon and Persia. Due to poor political choices, and their disobedience to God, Israel was taken captive.

After the Israelites returned to Israel from exile, they saw the rise of Greece under the leadership of Alexander the Great. Then followed by Syria led by Antiochus IV who imposed laws to keep Israel from worshiping God. Then, setting the stage for the New Testament, Rome took over and the people were oppressed under King Herod who was placed over Israel.

Israel needed a savior.

JOHN: THE BAPTIZER

> *In the time of Herod king of Judea there was a priest named Zechariah, who belonged to the priestly division of Abijah; his wife Elizabeth was also a descendant of Aaron. Both of them were righteous in the sight of God, observing all the Lord's commands and decrees blamelessly. But they were childless because Elizabeth was not able to conceive, and they were both very old. Luke 1:5-7 NIV*

At Elizabeth's age, her infertility had most likely forced her into the belief that having biological children was not an option. But even in their childlessness their faith didn't waver.

But because of this couple's righteousness, God chose them for a great task.

> *"Do not be afraid, Zechariah; your prayer has been heard. Your wife Elizabeth will bear you a son, and you are to call him John. He will be a joy and delight to you, and many will rejoice because of his birth, for he will be great in the sight of the Lord. He is never to take wine or other fermented drink, and he will be filled with the Holy Spirit even before he is born. He will bring back many of the people of Israel to the Lord their God. And he will go on before the Lord . . . to make ready a people prepared for the Lord." Luke 1:13-17 NIV*

Their son's name would be John. But, you might know him as John the Baptist. He would be the one to prepare the way for Jesus.

JESUS' BIRTH

Throughout the Old Testament we spoke about The Gift. Remember make babies and protect the land? Israel had gone in circles with this concept and continually failed. Don't get me wrong . . . they made babies. But they failed to protect the land and keep it holy. The other nations became leaders and Israel became their follower. The world needed to be redeemed. This was a much larger conversation than just about Israel. So, God gave them a new gift—Jesus. He would be the ultimate sacrifice to cleanse the entire world.

> *In the sixth month of Elizabeth's pregnancy, God sent the angel Gabriel to Nazareth, a town in Galilee, to a virgin pledged to be married to a man named Joseph, a descendant of David. The virgin's name was Mary. The angel went to her and said, "Greetings, you who are highly favored! The Lord is with you." Mary was greatly troubled at his words and wondered what kind of greeting this might be. But the angel said to her, "Do not be afraid, Mary; you have found favor with God. You will conceive and give birth to a son, and you are to call him Jesus. He will be great and will be called the Son of the Most High. The Lord God will give him the throne of his father David, and he will reign over Jacob's descendants forever; his kingdom will never end."*
>
> *"How will this be," Mary asked the angel, "since I am a virgin?"*

The angel answered, "The Holy Spirit will come on you, and the power of the Most High will overshadow you. So the holy one to be born will be called the Son of God."

"I am the Lord's servant," Mary answered. "May your word to me be fulfilled." Then the angel left her. Luke 1:26-35, 38 NIV

Because Joseph her husband was faithful to the law, and yet did not want to expose her to public disgrace, he had in mind to divorce her quietly. But after he had considered this, an angel of the Lord appeared to him in a dream and said, "Joseph son of David, do not be afraid to take Mary home as your wife, because what is conceived in her is from the Holy Spirit. She will give birth to a son, and you are to give him the name Jesus, because he will save his people from their sins."

All this took place to fulfill what the Lord had said through the prophet: "The virgin will conceive and give birth to a son, and they will call him Immanuel" (which means "God with us").

When Joseph woke up, he did what the angel of the Lord had commanded him and took Mary home as his wife. But he did not consummate their marriage until she gave birth to a son. And he gave him the name Jesus. Matthew 1:19-25 NIV

In those days Caesar Augustus issued a decree that a census should be taken of the entire Roman world. And everyone went to their own town to register. So Joseph also went up from the town of Nazareth in Galilee to Judea, to Bethlehem the town of David, because he belonged to the house and line of David. He went there to register with Mary, who was pledged to be married to him and was expecting a child. While they were there, the time came for the baby to be born, and she

> *gave birth to her firstborn, a son. She wrapped him in cloths and placed him in a manger, because there was no guest room available for them. Luke 2:1-7 NIV*

Jesus, the Son of God, came to earth as an infant. He wasn't born in a fancy home, but in a manger where animals lay, all because there was no room for Him elsewhere. The Savior of the world had arrived, yet the world didn't have a place for Him.

Sounds about right.

After Jesus' birth, the Magi came before King Herod and asked where to find Jesus, *the king of the Jews*. When he heard this, he was angry! King Herod felt he was the king! Was someone trying to rival him? He gathered the priests and teachers of the law and asked them where this messiah was born and they replied Bethlehem as it is written in the book of Micah. Herod tried to trick the Magi into finding Jesus for him but once they found Him, God warned them not to share their location. Then an Angel of the Lord told Joseph to get up and escape to Egypt for King Herod was going to try to kill Jesus. But after Herod's death they returned in peace.

PREPARING THE WAY

JESUS IN THE TEMPLE. Every year Mary and Joseph went to Jerusalem for the Festival of the Passover. When Jesus was twelve years old, they went to the festival as they routinely did, but when it was time to leave they left Jesus behind. They traveled an entire day's journey before realizing He wasn't with them. They must have had a massive caravan because they looked among their relatives and friends but He was nowhere to be found. They returned to Jerusalem as fast as they could and found Him after searching for three days.

Where was He? Sitting among the teachers in mid-discussion. The people were amazed at Jesus' understanding of the Holy Scriptures. But his parents were furious with Him.

> "Why were you searching for me? Didn't you know I had to be in my Father's house?" Luke 2:49 NIV

But they didn't understand what Jesus meant. They traveled back home and Jesus was obedient to them. Jesus continued to grow in stature and in relationship with humanity and with God.

JOHN THE BAPTIST. The Word of God came to John in the wilderness and told him to prepare the way for the Lord.

> As it is written in the book of the words of Isaiah the prophet: A voice of one calling in the wilderness, "Prepare the way for the Lord, make straight paths for him. Every valley shall be filled in, every mountain and hill made low. The crooked roads shall become straight, the rough ways smooth. And all people will see God's salvation." Luke 3:4-6 NIV

John preached to the crowds of good deeds and against social injustice. Many came to him and were baptized.

> The people were waiting expectantly and were all wondering in their hearts if John might possibly be the Messiah. John answered them all, "I baptize you with water. But one who is more powerful than

> I will come, the straps of whose sandals I am not worthy to untie. He will baptize you with the Holy Spirit and fire." Luke 3:15-16 NIV

JESUS' BAPTISM. *Then Jesus came from Galilee to the Jordan to be baptized by John. But John tried to deter him, saying, "I need to be baptized by you, and do you come to me?"*

> Jesus replied, "Let it be so now; it is proper for us to do this to fulfill all righteousness." Then John consented. As soon as Jesus was baptized, he went up out of the water. At that moment heaven was opened, and he saw the Spirit of God descending like a dove and alighting on him. And a voice from heaven said, "This is my Son, whom I love; with him I am well pleased." Matthew 3:13-17 NIV

When the decision to enter into a covenant relationship with God is made, it can almost feel as if you are walking into a warzone between God and Satan. It's almost as if you are holding God's hand as Satan is trying to pull you away. Jesus' baptism didn't look any different.

> Then Jesus was led by the Spirit into the wilderness to be tempted by the devil. After fasting forty days and forty nights, he was hungry.
>
> *Satan:* "If you are the Son of God, tell these stones to become bread."
>
> *Jesus:* "It is written: 'Man shall not live on bread alone, but on every word that comes from the mouth of God.'"
>
> Then the devil took him to the holy city and had him stand on the highest point of the temple.

Satan: "If you are the Son of God, throw yourself down. For it is written: 'He will command his angels concerning you, and they will lift you up in their hands, so that you will not strike your foot against a stone.'"

Jesus: "It is also written: 'Do not put the Lord your God to the test.'"

Again, the devil took him to a very high mountain and showed him all the kingdoms of the world and their splendor.

Satan: "All this I will give you, if you will bow down and worship me."

Jesus: "Away from me, Satan! For it is written: 'Worship the Lord your God, and serve him only." Then the devil left him, and angels came and attended him. Luke 4:1-11 NIV*

Did you notice the battle of the Scriptures at the end? Satan knows the Holy Scriptures, but Jesus breathed them. No temptation is too unbearable for Jesus.

JESUS' EARTHLY MINISTRY

CALLING OF THE APOSTLES. *Now Jesus himself was about thirty years old when he began his ministry. Luke 3:23 NIV*

Jesus began teaching in the synagogues and word quickly spread of His teaching and everyone praised Him.

Not much of Jesus' early life is recorded in scripture. But what we do have is mostly the last three years of His life. When He was thirty, He began teaching and found twelve men to journey with Him through ministry. And it was during these three years that Jesus poured a lifetime of wisdom into these men with one goal: Go be fishers of men.

(Side Note: These men weren't anything special. They were common people just like us. Throughout the entire story of the Bible God uses people like Noah (drunk), David (adulterer/murderer), Solomon (sex addict), Paul (formerly persecuted Christians), to do great things for His Kingdom. If you feel you have little to offer God . . . He will turn your gift into something greater!)

> As Jesus was walking beside the Sea of Galilee, he saw two brothers, Simon called Peter and his brother Andrew. They were casting a net into the lake, for they were fishermen. "Come, follow me," Jesus said, "and I will send you out to fish for people." At once they left their nets and followed him.
>
> Going on from there, he saw two other brothers, James son of Zebedee and his brother John. They were in a boat with their father Zebedee, preparing their nets. Jesus called them, and immediately they left the boat and their father and followed him. Matthew 4:18-22 NIV
>
> After this, Jesus went out and saw a tax collector by the name of Levi sitting at his tax booth. "Follow me," Jesus said to him, and Levi got up, left everything and followed him.
>
> Then Levi held a great banquet for Jesus at his house, and a large crowd of tax collectors and others were eating with them. But the Pharisees and the teachers of the law who belonged to their sect complained to his disciples, "Why do you eat and drink with tax collectors and sinners?" Jesus answered them, "It is not the healthy who need

> *a doctor, but the sick. I have not come to call the righteous, but sinners to repentance."*
> Luke 5:27-32 NIV

These are the names of the apostles Jesus called: Simon (Renamed Peter), Andrew, James, John, Philip, Thaddeus (also known as Jude), Bartholomew, Thomas, James (the lesser), Matthew (also known as Levi), Simon and Judas.

WHO PAID JESUS' BILLS? But it didn't stop with the twelve apostles. Jesus preached to massive groups of people in His time on earth and many of them tagged along for the ride. Jesus and His crew lived on the road and traveled all over Israel. Which brings us to the question: Who paid for their food, lodging and clothing?

> *After this, Jesus traveled about from one town and village to another, proclaiming the good news of the kingdom of God. The Twelve were with him, and also some women who had been cured of evil spirits and diseases: Mary (called Magdalene) from whom seven demons had come out; Joanna the wife of Chuza, the manager of Herod's household; Susanna; and many others. These women were helping to support them out of their own means.* Luke 8:1-3 NIV

Let's not jump to the conclusion that these three women paid all of the bills, but it was important enough to be mentioned in scripture. Mary Magdalene is mentioned in scripture as a repentant sinner who washed Jesus' feet with perfume and bore witness to the death, burial and resurrection of Jesus. Susanna is only mentioned in the scripture above. But Joanna was the wife of Chuza who worked for King Herod's son, Herod Antipas. Therefore,

Herod was indirectly funding the work of Jesus whom his father wanted dead.

THE FIRST MIRACLE. After Jesus had gathered His first followers they were all invited along with Jesus' mother Mary to a wedding in Cana of Galilee. Everyone was enjoying the wedding feast and apparently so much that the stock of wine had been depleted. This would have been embarrassing for the family of the bride and groom, so Mary turned to Jesus.

> *"Woman, why do you involve me?" Jesus replied. "My hour has not yet come." His mother said to the servants, "Do whatever he tells you." Nearby stood six stone water jars, the kind used by the Jews for ceremonial washing, each holding from twenty to thirty gallons. Jesus said to the servants, "Fill the jars with water"; so they filled them to the brim. Then he told them, "Now draw some out and take it to the master of the banquet." John 2:4-8 NIV*

The servants did as Jesus asked, and guess what! The wine was extravagant! The person in charge of the banquet pulled the groom aside and asked, *we usually give out the good stuff first and after the people are a little tipsy we give them the cheap stuff. They don't even notice by that point! But, you've saved the best until now!*

The Scripture doesn't even give us more context to the story. The writer just expects us to understand, *Yes, Jesus is just that good! No more explanation.*

SERMON ON THE MOUNT. After news got out that Jesus could perform miracles crowds began to form. One day as people were going to Jesus to be healed the crowd got so large that Jesus went up on a mountainside and spoke to the crowd. There were people from Galilee, Decapolis, Jerusalem, Judea and even from outside of Israel! The place was packed with people and Jesus didn't even have to lure them with donuts and coffee!

He looked out to the captive audience and began to speak deep truths to them. He didn't start out with a joke. He didn't keep it light. He dove right in with the hard stuff.

> *"Blessed are the poor in spirit, for theirs is the kingdom of heaven. Blessed are those who mourn, for they will be comforted. Blessed are the meek, for they will inherit the earth.*
>
> *Blessed are you when people insult you, persecute you and falsely say all kinds of evil against you because of me. Rejoice and be glad, because great is your reward in heaven, for in the same way they persecuted the prophets who were before you."*
> Matthew 5:3-5, 11-12 NIV

Many of these people were meeting Jesus for the first time and He was telling them things such as *you are the light of the world; do not murder; do not commit adultery; love your enemies; be honest with others; and give to the needy*. Jesus shared with them how to pray and how to live a holy life. These people may not have known Jesus, but He knew them and cared about them.

But He didn't stop there. Jesus spoke spiritual truths throughout His ministry. He was finally among humanity in the flesh. He had a lot to say.

Some was said in parables and others were told in great sermons in synagogues, mountainsides or while fishing in a boat. His time with humanity was limited but He preached with every breath and in every conversation. And His constant message was this: be holy and live up to your calling.

Jesus is God. He knew the people's hearts extremely well, as He knows ours today. He knew what the people were capable of and wanted to guide them to become great!

Jesus knew the religious Law and the people's obsession with keeping it. He wrote the Law! He didn't come to abolish the Law but He came as the fulfillment of the Law. His aim was to bring the people's eyes off the religious obsession and place their focus on Him. And in focusing on Him the people would find order in the chaos that was the world at that time.

THE GREAT. THE MEEK. THE MULTITUDE. Jesus walked among the greatest and the least in the world. In His all-encompassing wisdom, He viewed the people all the same. Everyone was broken and everyone needed Him.

NICODEMUS. Due to all of the hype about Jesus, the religious leaders caught wind of him. There was a Pharisee named Nicodemus who came to Jesus one night. As a Pharisee, he was a pretty powerful guy. He saw Jesus and recognized the miracles He performed and knew He had to be from God. And right off the bat they begin discussing deep theological concepts such as eternal life.

THE WOMAN AND THE SICK. But Jesus didn't only speak with the greats. One day as Jesus and His disciples were traveling Jesus stopped in a village of Samaria (a place looked down upon by the rest of Israel). There He sat at a well beside a woman in the heat of the day. This woman had been married several times and was then living with her boyfriend. She had lived a pretty rough life and Jesus wanted to sit with her. The woman's focus was on her life, but Jesus spoke to her eternity and purpose.

After their conversation the woman went back to her village and told the people that she'd met the Messiah. And because of her faith many in her village met Jesus and believed in Him.

Jesus cared for the broken. He healed people of evil spirits; raised the dead; cured leprosy, paralytics, blindness and deafness. We even find Jesus healing a soldier's severed ear during His later arrest. The guy was a saint (well, actually He *is* God).

FEEDING THE 5,000. Jesus even spoke to the multitude. One day while Jesus was out in a boat in a solitary place mourning the loss of His cousin John the Baptist who had been killed in ministry, crowds found him and Jesus had compassion on them. If this doesn't tell us that God takes time for us, I don't know what will. They brought their sick to Him and He healed them.

> *As evening approached, the disciples came to him and said, "This is a remote place, and it's already getting late. Send the crowds away, so they can go to the villages and buy themselves some food." Jesus replied, "They do not need to go away. You give them something to eat. "We have here only five loaves of bread and two fish," they answered. "Bring them here to me," he said. And he directed the people to sit down on the grass. Taking the five loaves and the two fish and looking up to heaven, he gave thanks and broke the loaves. Then he gave them to the disciples, and the disciples gave*

them to the people. They all ate and were satisfied, and the disciples picked up twelve basketfuls of broken pieces that were left over. The number of those who ate was about five thousand men, besides women and children." Matthew 14:15-21 NIV

PHARISEES. Jesus' ministry was expanding and He was doing great things throughout Israel, but the Pharisees didn't approve of it. They viewed Him as a heretic because His teachings didn't line up with their way of religion.

Who were the Pharisees anyway? Between the Old and New Testaments we see the rise of religion in Israel led by two religious sects: Pharisees and Sadducees. Can you blame them? The Israelites knew their history. God called Israel to obey Him continuously and they continued to fail. Their consequence was exile. Israel lost their land and God's temple. They didn't want that to happen again!

Though these groups were most likely created to aid in religious order they became so obsessed with laws that their focus became set on religion more so than on God. And it was that place that humanity found themselves in that lured them to want to kill the Savior of the world.

THE FINAL WEEK

TRIUMPHAL ENTRY. Jesus' time on earth was coming to a close, but His mission was not yet complete.

Israel knew of a Messiah who would come and save them from their bondage. The Old Testament prophets foretold this news long before Jesus was born in Bethlehem.

But Israel expected a grand king who would set up their throne and ride on a chariot. Yet what they got was a servant who rode a donkey.

> As they approached Jerusalem and came to Bethphage on the Mount of Olives, Jesus sent two disciples, saying to them, "Go to the village ahead of you, and at once you will find a donkey tied there, with her colt by her. Untie them and bring them to me. If anyone says anything to you, say that the Lord needs them, and he will send them right away."
>
> They brought the donkey and the colt and placed their cloaks on them for Jesus to sit on. A very large crowd spread their cloaks on the road, while others cut branches from the trees and spread them on the road. The crowds that went ahead of him and those that followed shouted, "Hosanna to the Son of David! Blessed is he who comes in the name of the Lord! Hosanna in the highest heaven!" When Jesus entered Jerusalem, the whole city was stirred and asked, "Who is this?" The crowds answered, "This is Jesus, the prophet from Nazareth in Galilee." Matthew 21:1-3, 7-11 NIV

CLEARING THE TEMPLE. *On reaching Jerusalem, Jesus entered the temple courts and began driving out those who were buying and selling there. He overturned the tables of the money changers and the benches of those selling doves, and would not allow anyone to carry merchandise through the temple courts. And as he taught them, he said, "Is it not written: 'My house will be called a house of prayer for all nations'? But you have made it 'a den of robbers.'" Mark 11:15-17 NIV*

> The blind and the lame came to him at the temple, and he healed them. But when the chief priests and the teachers of the law saw the won-

> derful things he did and the children shouting in the temple courts, "Hosanna to the Son of David," they were indignant. Matthew 21:14-15 NIV

Jesus was fed up with the order of His temple. The status of the temple greatly represented the state of Israel: deceitful. But beauty is found in what happened the moment Jesus began to cleanse the temple. The blind and lame came to Jesus and they were healed. That's the purpose of the temple, for humanity to come before God.

But the reasoning for cleansing the temple didn't end there. The people were using the courts of the Gentiles as the market place. The place God had designed for people outside of Israel to come worship and sacrifice had become an over-priced market (or den of robbers. That sounds more cool).

THE PLOT TO KILL JESUS. The religious leaders didn't like Jesus very much. He didn't fit the mold that they'd pictured as the Messiah, so they didn't believe He was whom He said He was. But I'd imagine Jesus' act at the temple was the last straw. They wanted Jesus dead.

> Then the chief priests and the elders of the people assembled in the palace of the high priest, whose name was Caiaphas, and they schemed to arrest Jesus secretly and kill him.
>
> Then one of the Twelve—the one called Judas Iscariot—went to the chief priests and asked, "What are you willing to give me if I deliver him over to you?" So they counted out for him thirty pieces of silver. From then on Judas watched for an opportunity to hand him over. Matthew 26:3-4; 14-16 NIV

THE LAST SUPPER. Jesus knew His time with the apostles was coming to an end so He gathered them together for one last meal.

But before they ate, Jesus did something radical. It was custom for the servant of the house to wash the feet of a guest when they enter the home. Sandals were the norm so people's feet got pretty dirty. In a bold move, Jesus took the place of a servant and washed the disciples' feet.

"Do you understand what I have done for you?" he asked them. You call me 'Teacher' and 'Lord,' and rightly so, for that is what I am. Now that I, your Lord and Teacher, have washed your feet, you also should wash one another's feet. I have set you an example that you should do as I have done for you. Very truly I tell you, no servant is greater than his master, nor is a messenger greater than the one who sent him. Now that you know these things, you will be blessed if you do them. John 13:12-17 NIV

While they were eating, Jesus took bread, and when he had given thanks, he broke it and gave it to his disciples, saying, "Take and eat; this is my body." Then he took a cup, and when he had given thanks, he gave it to them, saying, "Drink from it, all of you. This is my blood of the covenant, which is poured out for many for the forgiveness of sins. I tell you, I will not drink from this fruit of the vine from now on until that day when I drink it new with you in my Father's kingdom." Matthew 26:26-29 NIV

"My children, I will be with you only a little longer. You will look for me, and just as I told the Jews, so I tell you now: Where I am going, you cannot come. A new command I give you: Love one another. As I have loved you, so you must love one another. By this everyone will know that you are my disciples, if you love one another." Simon Peter asked

> him, "Lord, where are you going?" Jesus replied, "Where I am going, you cannot follow now, but you will follow later." John 13:33-36 NIV

Can you even imagine the emotional nature of this meal? Jesus informed the apostles that He would soon no longer be with them but that He would send His Spirit to live in those who believe in Him. Jesus revealed His death to the apostles several times throughout His ministry but they never fully understood Him. Very soon it would become a reality for them.

JESUS' ARREST. After they ate, Jesus led the apostles just outside of Jerusalem to the Mount of Olives where He spent many nights (Luke 21:37). Knowing this habit, Judas Iscariot knew exactly where Jesus would be at that hour.

> While he was still speaking, Judas, one of the Twelve, arrived. With him was a large crowd armed with swords and clubs, sent from the chief priests and the elders of the people. Now the betrayer had arranged a signal with them: "The one I kiss is the man; arrest him." Going at once to Jesus, Judas said, "Greetings, Rabbi!" and kissed him.
>
> Jesus replied, "Do what you came for, friend."
>
> Then the men stepped forward, seized Jesus and arrested him. Matthew 26:47-50 NIV

Peter cut off a soldier's ear (and Jesus healed it!) The apostles fled! Jesus was arrested! But during all of this, Jesus was peaceful.

JESUS ON TRIAL. After they arrested Jesus, they took Him before the religious leaders and were brutal. They mocked Him, hit Him and spit in His face.

God was on trial and it was a nasty sight.

> *The chief priests and the whole Sanhedrin were looking for false evidence against Jesus so that they could put him to death. But they did not find any, though many false witnesses came forward. Finally two came forward and declared, "This fellow said, 'I am able to destroy the temple of God and rebuild it in three days.'"*
>
> *Then the high priest stood up and said to Jesus, "Are you not going to answer? What is this testimony that these men are bringing against you?" But Jesus remained silent.*
>
> *The high priest said to him, "I charge you under oath by the living God: Tell us if you are the Messiah, the Son of God."*
>
> *"You have said so," Jesus replied. "But I say to all of you: From now on you will see the Son of Man sitting at the right hand of the Mighty One and coming on the clouds of heaven."*
>
> *Then the high priest tore his clothes and said, "He has spoken blasphemy! Why do we need any more witnesses? Look, now you have heard the blasphemy. What do you think?" "He is worthy of death," they answered.*
>
> *Then they spit in his face and struck him with their fists. Others slapped him and said, "Prophesy to us, Messiah. Who hit you?" Matthew 26:59-68 NIV*

The religious leaders didn't have the legal capability to execute Jesus, so they turned Jesus over to the government.

> Early in the morning, all the chief priests and the elders of the people made their plans how to have Jesus executed. So they bound him, led him away and handed him over to Pilate the governor. Matthew 27:1-2 NIV
>
> Jesus stood before the governor, and the governor asked him, "Are you the king of the Jews?"
>
> "You have said so," Jesus replied.
>
> When he was accused by the chief priests and the elders, he gave no answer. Then Pilate asked him, "Don't you hear the testimony they are bringing against you?" But Jesus made no reply, not even to a single charge—to the great amazement of the governor.

(Pilate wasn't a Jew. He was a Roman official serving his role as Governor in Jerusalem. Jesus was no threat to him, so he wanted to find a way to release Jesus but still stay on the Jews' good side.)

> Now it was the governor's custom at the festival to release a prisoner chosen by the crowd. At that time they had a well-known prisoner whose name was Jesus Barabbas. So when the crowd had gathered, Pilate asked them, "Which one do you want me to release to you: Jesus Barabbas, or Jesus who is called the Messiah?"
>
> While Pilate was sitting on the judge's seat, his wife sent him this message: "Don't have anything to do with that innocent man, for I have suffered a great deal today in a dream because of him." But the chief priests and the elders persuaded the crowd to ask for Barabbas and to have Jesus executed. "Which of the two do you want me to release to you?" asked the governor. "Barabbas," they answered. "What shall I do, then, with Jesus who is

called the Messiah?" Pilate asked. They all answered, "Crucify him!" "Why? What crime has he committed?" asked Pilate. But they shouted all the louder, "Crucify him!"

When Pilate saw that he was getting nowhere, but that instead an uproar was starting, he took water and washed his hands in front of the crowd. "I am innocent of this man's blood," he said. "It is your responsibility!" All the people answered, "His blood is on us and on our children!" Then he released Barabbas to them. But he had Jesus flogged, and handed him over to be crucified. 27:11-26 NIV

CRUCIFIXION. *Then the governor's soldiers took Jesus into the Praetorium and gathered the whole company of soldiers around him. They stripped him and put a scarlet robe on him, and then twisted together a crown of thorns and set it on his head. They put a staff in his right hand. Then they knelt in front of him and mocked him. "Hail, king of the Jews!" they said. They spit on him, and took the staff and struck him on the head again and again. After they had mocked him, they took off the robe and put his own clothes on him. Then they led him away to crucify him.*

As they were going out, they met a man from Cyrene, named Simon, and they forced him to carry the cross. They came to a place called Golgotha (which means "the place of the skull"). There they offered Jesus wine to drink, mixed with gall; but after tasting it, he refused to drink it. When they had crucified him, they divided up his clothes by casting lots. And sitting down, they kept watch over him there. Above his head they placed the written charge against him: THIS IS JESUS, KING OF THE JEWS.

From noon until three in the afternoon darkness came over all the land. About three in the after-

noon Jesus cried out in a loud voice, "Eli, Eli, lema sabachthani?" (which means "My God, my God, why have you forsaken me?"). When some of those standing there heard this, they said, "He's calling Elijah." Immediately one of them ran and got a sponge. He filled it with wine vinegar, put it on a staff, and offered it to Jesus to drink. The rest said, "Now leave him alone. Let's see if Elijah comes to save him." And when Jesus had cried out again in a loud voice, he gave up his spirit. At that moment the curtain of the temple was torn in two from top to bottom. The earth shook, the rocks split and the tombs broke open.

When the centurion and those with him who were guarding Jesus saw the earthquake and all that had happened, they were terrified, and exclaimed, "Surely he was the Son of God!" Many women were there, watching from a distance. They had followed Jesus from Galilee to care for his needs. Among them were Mary Magdalene, Mary the mother of James and Joseph, and the mother of Zebedee's sons. Matthew 27:27-37, 45-52, 54-56 NIV

And just like that, the final week of Jesus' life was finished. But in three days Jesus would come back to life with a gift for humanity: Eternal Life.

RESURRECTION. *After the Sabbath, at dawn on the first day of the week, Mary Magdalene and the other Mary went to look at the tomb. There was a violent earthquake, for an angel of the Lord came down from heaven and, going to the tomb, rolled back the stone and sat on it. His appearance was like lightning, and his clothes were white as snow. The guards were so afraid of him that they shook and became like dead men.*

The angel said to the women, "Do not be afraid, for I know that you are looking for Jesus, who was

> *crucified. He is not here; he has risen, just as he said. Come and see the place where he lay. Then go quickly and tell his disciples: 'He has risen from the dead and is going ahead of you into Galilee. There you will see him.' Now I have told you."*
>
> *So the women hurried away from the tomb, afraid yet filled with joy, and ran to tell his disciples. Suddenly Jesus met them. "Greetings," he said. They came to him, clasped his feet and worshiped him. Then Jesus said to them, "Do not be afraid. Go and tell my brothers to go to Galilee; there they will see me." Matthew 28:1-7 NIV*

After Jesus' resurrection He appeared and comforted many of his family and friends but reminded them of His purpose.

> *Some of the guards went into the city and reported to the chief priests everything that had happened. When the chief priests had met with the elders and devised a plan, they gave the soldiers a large sum of money, telling them, "You are to say, 'His disciples came during the night and stole him away while we were asleep.' If this report gets to the governor, we will satisfy him and keep you out of trouble." So the soldiers took the money and did as they were instructed. And this story has been widely circulated among the Jews to this very day. Matthew 28:11-15 NIV*

THE GREAT COMMISSION. Jesus' purpose for coming to earth had almost come to a close. Before leaving His apostles he had one final matter to take care of. Things were going to soon look very different. The temple would be destroyed and the hub of Christianity would no longer be found in a building but in the souls of every believer through the Holy Spirit. Every nation would be reached with the story of Christ and all would be invited in.

> *Then Jesus came to the disciples and said, "All authority in heaven and on earth has been given to me. Therefore go and make disciples of all nations, baptizing them in the name of the Father and of the Son and of the Holy Spirit, and teaching them to obey everything I have commanded you. And surely I am with you always, to the very end of the age." Matthew 28:17-20 NIV*

Jesus' mission was accomplished, but in many ways it had just begun. Now, on to the vehicle that would carry out this plan.

CHURCH

CHAPTER FOURTEEN

But you will receive power when the Holy Spirit has come upon you, and you will be my witnesses in Jerusalem and in all Judea and Samaria, and to the end of the earth.
Acts 1:8 NIV

THE NEW BEGINNING

AND THEN THERE WERE TWELVE. The four gospels (Matthew, Mark, Luke, and John) ends with Jesus' ascension into Heaven and Acts opens with Jesus' final words.

> *"You will receive power when the Holy Spirit comes on you; and you will be my witnesses in Jerusalem, and in all Judea and Samaria, and to the ends of the earth." After he said this, he was taken up before their very eyes, and a cloud hid him from their sight. Acts 1:8-9 NIV*

The apostles replaced Judas Iscariot after his betrayal of Jesus with another follower of Jesus named Matthias and then the church exploded in numbers! First of all in Jewish circles and then in Gentile circles through Paul's ministry and others within the church expanding throughout the Roman world. And much of the book of Acts traces the spreading of the gospel through the ministries of Peter and Paul and a few others until the gospel is actually well established in Rome itself (AKA the super power at that time).

When the day of Pentecost came, all the apostles were together in a house, and a sound like a violent wind from heaven filled it. They looked around as they saw something like fiery tongues resting on each of them.

Crowds of people came together in awe of what was happening. People from different nations were able to understand each other in their own language. Others watched as they assumed everyone was drunk! But Peter addressed the crowd by quoting the words of God in the book of Joel.

> *"I will pour out my Spirit on all people. Your sons and daughters will prophesy, your old men will dream dreams, your young men will see visions. Even on my servants, both men and women, I will pour out my Spirit in those days. I will show wonders in the heavens and on the earth, blood and fire and billows of smoke. The sun will be turned to darkness and the moon to blood before the coming of the great and dreadful day of the Lord. And everyone who calls on the name of the Lord will be saved."*
> *Joel 2:28-32 NIV*

(Side note: Pentecost was fifty days after the first Sunday following the Passover. In other words, it had been a while since Jesus' ascension.)

And with a captive audience, Peter began to explain to the crowd that Jesus is truly God and that *they* put Him to death. Peter's words touched the crowd and they began to ask what they should do. And Peter replied, *repent and be baptized! Your sins will be forgiven and you will receive the Holy Spirit.* About three thousand people gave their lives to Christ that day.

The apostles took Jesus' great commission to heart. They spread out and began teaching, healing and baptizing and the number of believers continued to grow by the thousands.

But this didn't stop the religious leaders from trying to tear Jesus' ministry apart. The apostles were persecuted and imprisoned for their faith. And it didn't end with the apostles. Jesus taught, healed and cared for a lot of people who dedicated their life to following Him as one of His disciples. Among those disciples was a man named Stephen who was a man full of God's grace and yet killed for his faith.

I remember a time when our churches would pray consistently with thanksgiving for the United States being a place free from spiritual persecution. But sadly, today persecution makes our world a scary place.

SAUL BEFORE PAUL

The Pharisees were brutal in their persecution of Jesus' followers. They were ruthless in their attempt to erase Jesus' name from history. They hated Jesus that much. There was one Pharisee whose hatred seemed to rise above the rest and his name was Saul. Saul was the son of a Pharisee groomed in the arts of his father.

Saul was there in the stoning of Stephen. He was actually the one who called the shot. Saul went out of his way to persecute Christians.

> *Saul began to destroy the church. Going from house to house, he dragged off both men and women and put them in prison. Acts 8:3 NIV*

The church became scattered in its persecution, but everyone preached wherever they went and people listened.

Saul was good at what he did. But he was using his talents against God rather than for Him. One day as he was traveling to Damascus to continue persecuting Christians, he was stopped by a bright light and he fell to the ground.

> *Jesus: "Saul, Saul, why do you persecute me?"*
>
> *Saul: "Who are you, Lord?"*
>
> *Jesus: "I am Jesus, whom you are persecuting. Now get up and go into the city, and you will be told what you must do." Acts 9:4-6 NIV*

Saul stood up, but he couldn't see. So his men led him into Damascus and for three days he ate or drank nothing. The man was in shock.

Now in the town lived a disciple of Jesus by the name of Ananias whom Jesus called to heal Saul.

(Side Note: Ananias wanted nothing to do with Saul because he knew Saul's story. But God had a better story for Saul.)

God changed his name to Paul and gave him the calling to proclaim Jesus' name to the Gentiles (AKA, those outside Israel). Paul's new life didn't start out easy. The Jews didn't like his change of heart and tried to kill him. He tried to join the disciples but they were scared of him and didn't trust him until a man named Barnabas introduced them and shared Paul's conversion story. But he carried on and continued to preach the gospel everywhere he went.

PAUL'S MISSIONARY JOURNEYS

As a Pharisee, Paul was very zealous with his faith. That charisma wasn't lost when he became a Christ follower. If he was going to do something, he gave it everything he had. After Paul's conversion, he spent the rest of his life spreading the story of Jesus to those outside of Israel. His ministry can be summed up in three missionary journeys.

(1.0) Paul and Barnabas (the guy who introduced him to the apostles after his conversion) left Israel and spent months spreading the gospel in modern Turkey and Syria. They would visit Jewish synagogues and teach both Jews and Gentiles about Jesus.

> *"Fellow Israelites and you Gentiles who worship God, listen to me! The God of the people of Israel chose our ancestors; he made the people prosper during their stay in Egypt; with mighty power he led them out of that country; for about forty years he endured their conduct in the wilderness; and he overthrew seven nations in Canaan, giving their land to his people as their inheritance. All this took about 450 years.*

After this, God gave them judges until the time of Samuel the prophet. Then the people asked for a king, and he gave them Saul son of Kish, of the tribe of Benjamin, who ruled forty years. After removing Saul, he made David their king. God testified concerning him: 'I have found David son of Jesse, a man after my own heart; he will do everything I want him to do.'

From this man's descendants God has brought to Israel the Savior Jesus, as he promised. Before the coming of Jesus, John preached repentance and baptism to all the people of Israel. As John was completing his work, he said: 'Who do you suppose I am? I am not the one you are looking for. But there is one coming after me whose sandals I am not worthy to untie.'

Fellow children of Abraham and you God-fearing Gentiles, it is to us that this message of salvation has been sent. The people of Jerusalem and their rulers did not recognize Jesus, yet in condemning him they fulfilled the words of the prophets that are read every Sabbath. Though they found no proper ground for a death sentence, they asked Pilate to have him executed. When they had carried out all that was written about him, they took him down from the cross and laid him in a tomb. But God raised him from the dead, and for many days he was seen by those who had traveled with him from Galilee to Jerusalem. They are now his witnesses to our people.

We tell you the good news: What God promised our ancestors he has fulfilled for us, their children, by raising up Jesus." Acts 13:16-33 NIV

But, in the midst of their efforts, Jews would follow behind them and challenge their teachings. Good thing Paul and Barnabas knew the Old Testament, because they shot back,

> "I have made you a light for the Gentiles, that you may bring salvation to the ends of the earth.'" Acts 13:47 NIV (in reference to Isaiah 49:6)

(2.0). After their first missionary journey, Paul and Barnabas split up and they both took assistants: Paul took Silas and Barnabas took his nephew Mark.

(Side Note: This was the same Mark who wrote the Gospel of Mark.)

After splitting up, Paul and Silas met a young man named Timothy and visited a lot of the same people Paul had met on his first missionary journey. That was probably his original plan, but God had a different plan.

After trying to go their own way, the Spirit of Jesus led them to Greece.

First they met a store owner named Lydia in Philippi and baptized her entire family. Then Paul and Silas got thrown in prison for healing a demon-possessed girl (her owners were making money off of her fortune telling), but God released them from their chains and they continued to baptize and spread the gospel to places like Thessalonica, Berea, Athens, Corinth and Ephesus.

House churches began to develop and we find Paul being respectful of these cities' people and their culture. He brought the gospel as a seed and let it set root and blossom in their environment. The point wasn't to Judaize the world, but to bring Jesus to them. He made real relationships with the people in these cities. They celebrated together and mourned together. When it was time for Paul to leave these churches, there was sadness.

(3.0). After some time, Paul returned to minister to the churches for a final time. He put in place elders and leaders to help the churches strive. But this trip was different than the rest. Paul could sense through the Holy Spirit that there might not be another trip.

At the end of his trip Paul spoke to the elders of the church in Ephesus for he knew he wouldn't see them again.

> "You know how I lived the whole time I was with you, from the first day I came into the province of Asia. I served the Lord with great humility and with tears and in the midst of severe testing by the plots of my Jewish opponents. You know that I have not hesitated to preach anything that would be helpful to you but have taught you publicly and from house to house. I have declared to both Jews and Greeks that they must turn to God in repentance and have faith in our Lord Jesus.
>
> And now, compelled by the Spirit, I am going to Jerusalem, not knowing what will happen to me there. I only know that in every city the Holy Spirit warns me that prison and hardships are facing me. However, I consider my life worth nothing to me; my only aim is to finish the race and complete the task the Lord Jesus has given me—the task of testifying to the good news of God's grace.
>
> Now I know that none of you among whom I have gone about preaching the kingdom will ever see me again. Therefore, I declare to you today that I am innocent of the blood of any of you. For I have not hesitated to proclaim to you the whole will of God. Keep watch over yourselves and all the flock

> *of which the Holy Spirit has made you overseers. Be shepherds of the church of God, which he bought with his own blood." Acts 20:18-28 NIV*

FROM JERUSALEM TO ROME

Paul then set sail for Israel. It was his final return. When his boat hit the port in Caesarea, Israel a prophet named Agabus met him there and told him that he would soon be arrested in Jerusalem!

Talk about bearer of bad news.

After all the good that Paul had done, now this? Could the Jewish leaders really not understand that God just might in fact love the Gentiles too? His companions pleaded with him to run away from Israel, but Paul knew what he had to do. So they headed toward Jerusalem.

> *Some Jews from the province of Asia saw Paul at the temple. They stirred up the whole crowd and seized him, shouting, "Fellow Israelites, help us! This is the man who teaches everyone everywhere against our people and our law and this place. And besides, he has brought Greeks into the temple and defiled this holy place." Acts 21:27-28 NIV*

The entire city was in an uproar. Rioters seized Paul and tried to kill him. The officials saw the chaos and put chains on him. Crowds were screaming. The mob was so violent that soldiers had to carry Paul away and put him in barracks.

But before they put him away, Paul asked the commander if he could speak to the crowd. In the middle of an uproar Paul began to speak and the people listened.

He told his conversion story and the people listened until he told them that Jesus sent him to preach to the Gentiles. At that moment the crowd stirred up again and the command ordered for him to be brought to the barracks and be beaten.

Beaten? Paul had one trick up his sleeve. He was born a Roman citizen and it was illegal for a Roman citizen to be punished without a fair trial. So, Paul went on trial before the Sanhedrin (Jewish Religious Council); Governor Felix and then again by his successor Festus; and finally before King Agrippa.

No trial could find reason to put Paul to death but the Jews pursued so he appealed to Caesar. The final call was to send Paul to Rome for trial.

After a ship ride, a disastrous storm, and a shipwreck, Paul landed in Rome. He was put on house arrest and guarded by a soldier. But no hardship could keep Paul from spreading the gospel. For two years Paul stayed there and taught about Jesus.

THE LETTERS

CHAPTER FIFTEEN

Grace and peace to you from God our Father and the Lord Jesus Christ Galatians 1:3 NIV

During the apostles' ministry they made relationships with many different churches across the known world. Their best way of keeping in touch with these churches and building them up was through writing letters.

I love letters. There is something about getting out a piece of paper and a pen and just writing to someone you care about. When my wife and I were dating, we would write letters back and forth because she lived eight hours away. I wanted to keep up with her while she was away and there is just something special about seeing the person's handwriting that makes them feel just a little bit closer.

The authors of these letters below cared for the people to whom they were writing. The wonderful thing is we still have many of those letters and we get to read them!

JAMES. The brother of Jesus. The guy who grew up beside the Messiah. That alone should make us want to read his letter.

James wrote his letter after Jesus' disciples had just scattered in fear for their lives due to the great persecution of Christians in Jerusalem. James, being the leader of the Church in Jerusalem, sent word to the twelve tribes of Israel to strengthen them. His letter isn't very long but it's dense with spiritual truths.

> *"Consider it pure joy, my brothers and sisters, whenever you face trials of many kinds, because you know that the testing of your faith produces perseverance. Let perseverance finish its work so that you may be mature and complete, not lacking anything. If any of you lacks wisdom, you should ask God, who gives generously to all without finding fault, and it will be given to you." James 1:2-5 NIV*

> *"My dear brothers and sisters, take note of this: Everyone should be quick to listen, slow to speak and slow to become angry, because human anger does not produce the righteousness that God desires. Therefore, get rid of all moral filth and the evil that is so prevalent and humbly accept the word planted in you, which can save you. Do not merely listen to the word, and so deceive yourselves. Do what it says." James 1:19-22 NIV*

> *"Those who consider themselves religious and yet do not keep a tight rein on their tongues deceive themselves, and their religion is worthless. Religion that God our Father accepts as pure and faultless*

> is this: to look after orphans and widows in their distress and to keep oneself from being polluted by the world." James 1:26-27 NIV

> "What good is it, my brothers and sisters, if someone claims to have faith but has no deeds? Can such faith save them? Suppose a brother or a sister is without clothes and daily food. If one of you says to them, "Go in peace; keep warm and well fed," but does nothing about their physical needs, what good is it? In the same way, faith by itself, if it is not accompanied by action, is dead." 2:14-17 NIV

1 THESSALONIANS. As we read in the last chapter, Paul set up many churches on his missionary journeys. But once he left them, he didn't leave them high and dry. He wrote them letters and kept up with them giving them spiritual guidance.

Paul, along with Silas and Timothy, continuously praised the church in Thessalonica. Ministering to churches can be difficult. There are so many different people with various personalities and understandings of scripture. But here we find Paul's relationship with the church in Thessalonica to be flourishing.

Paul gave the church some encouraging words about Jesus' second coming and living a holy life in pursuit of that day.

> "Rejoice always, pray continually, give thanks in all circumstances; for this is God's will for you in Christ Jesus. Do not quench the Spirit. Do not treat prophecies with contempt but test them all; hold on to what is good, reject every kind of evil. May God himself, the God of peace, sanctify you through and through. May your whole spirit, soul and body

> be kept blameless at the coming of our Lord Jesus Christ." 1 Thessalonians 5:16-23 NIV

2 THESSALONIANS. Sometime after the church received Paul's first letter they became fearful of Jesus' second coming. *Has it already happened? Did we not make the cut?* Paul wrote Thessalonica another letter in hope to calm their fears and to set straight their doctrine of the Second Coming.

> "Don't let anyone deceive you in any way, for that day will not come until the rebellion occurs and the man of lawlessness is revealed, the man doomed to destruction. He will oppose and will exalt himself over everything that is called God or is worshiped, so that he sets himself up in God's temple, proclaiming himself to be God." 2 Thessalonians 2:3-4 NIV

1 CORINTHIANS. Paul began his letter in a fairly traditional way to the church in Corinth, but tagged on his title of apostleship. Paul stayed in Corinth for a year and a half on his second missionary journey . . . apparently the church had become divided and some of the church lost confidence in his authority. They were making religious leaders out to be politicians and choosing whom they wanted to follow.

> "One of you says, 'I follow Paul'; another, 'I follow Apollos'; another, 'I follow Cephas'; still another, 'I follow Christ.' Is Christ divided? Was Paul crucified for you? Were you baptized in the name of Paul?" 1 Corinthians 1:12-13 NIV

Paul didn't want any credit. Peter and Apollos didn't either. Their duty was to share with everyone the good news of Jesus and to explain how to live a holy life.

> "Now these things occurred as examples to keep us from setting our hearts on evil things as they did. Do not be idolaters, as some of them were; as it is written: 'The people sat down to eat and drink and got up to indulge in revelry.' We should not commit sexual immorality, as some of them did—and in one day twenty-three thousand of them died. We should not test Christ, as some of them did—and were killed by snakes. And do not grumble, as some of them did—and were killed by the destroying angel.
>
> These things happened to them as examples and were written down as warnings for us, on whom the culmination of the ages has come. So, if you think you are standing firm, be careful that you don't fall! No temptation has overtaken you except what is common to mankind. And God is faithful; he will not let you be tempted beyond what you can bear. But when you are tempted, he will also provide a way out so that you can endure it." 1 Corinthians 10:6-13 NIV

But if this holy life was going to be lived, something had be done about the division within their church. So Paul reminded them that they are one body baptized into one Spirit with one Christ. They should never divide what God had brought together.

The great thing about the body of Christ is that we have been given unique gifts. Some people are great with kids. Other people are fantastic at leading worship. A great number of people are incredible at teaching. These are all great things. But when it comes down to it, if we do good deeds but lack love . . . we've missed the point. Paul goes to the extent of if we were to give everything we own away to the poor and lack love it would be pointless.

GALATIANS. With this letter, Paul gets straight to the point. *There is NO OTHER GOSPEL than that of Christ Jesus.* Since Paul had left Galatia he learned that the gospel of Christ was being perverted.

> *"I want you to know, brothers and sisters, that the gospel I preached is not of human origin. I did not receive it from any man, nor was I taught it; rather, I received it by revelation from Jesus Christ." Galatians 1:11-12 NIV*

Paul's frustration stems from the Galatian's weak theology. He couldn't understand how he had spent hours telling them about the good news of Jesus and how they had so easily lost sight of what he had told them. Many in the church had gained a works-based theology instead of the faith-based theology that Paul had taught them.

> *"For all who rely on the works of the law are under a curse, as it is written: 'Cursed is everyone who does not continue to do everything written in the Book of the Law.' Clearly no one who relies on the law is justified before God, because 'the righteous will live by faith.' The law is not based on faith; on the contrary, it says, 'The person who does these things will live by them.' Christ redeemed us from the curse of the law" Galatians 3:10-13 NIV*

> *"You, my brothers and sisters, were called to be free. But do not use your freedom to indulge the flesh rather, serve one another humbly in love. For the entire law is fulfilled in keeping this one command: 'Love your neighbor as yourself.'" Galatians 5:13-14 NIV*

ROMANS. Paul longed to visit Rome throughout his ministry. Before getting the chance to actually visit Rome, he wrote the church a letter letting them know his desire to visit them and build them up. Romans is a letter about redemption and grace.

Paul launched early in his letter teaching the importance of living a holy life. Just like today, sin's grip is strong and Paul wanted to warn the church to fight against sin with righteousness.

> "The wrath of God is being revealed from heaven against all the godlessness and wickedness of people, who suppress the truth by their wickedness, since what may be known about God is plain to them, because God has made it plain to them. God will repay each person according to what they have done." Romans 1:18-19; 2:6 NIV

For thousands of years Jews were considered God's people. Paul's major audience on his missionary journeys were Gentile. How did Paul address this?

> "There is no difference between Jew and Gentile, for all have sinned and fall short of the glory of God, and all are justified freely by his grace through the redemption that came by Christ Jesus. God presented Christ as a sacrifice of atonement, through the shedding of his blood—to be received by faith." Romans 3:22-25 NIV

We are ONE in Christ! Jesus' death and resurrection wasn't just for Israel. It wasn't an act of selection. It was an act of unity! And we receive this grace by faith.

> "What shall we say, then? Shall we go on sinning so that grace may increase? By no means! We are those who have died to sin; how can we live in it any longer? Or don't you know that all of us who were baptized into Christ Jesus were baptized into his death? We were therefore buried with him through baptism into death in order that, just as Christ was raised from the dead through the glory of the Father, we too may live a new life." Romans 6:1-4 NIV

How do we live this new life? We are to live by the Spirit and not by the flesh. Our humanity draws us to look more like the world, but the Spirit draws us to look more like God.

2 CORINTHIANS. Paul's second letter to the church in Corinth was two-fold. He wanted the church to know that he was pleased with them for how they were striving to live godly lives, but it also served as a letter of defense for Paul.

Apparently, there were false teachers in Corinth who shoved Paul's name in the mud to make a greater name for themselves. They called him a terrible public speaker hoping to disqualify his message. But Paul wasn't going to let the gospel get lost in the false teachers' foolishness. In all of this, Paul continued to guide Corinth in the truth and built them up.

EPHESIANS. In the last chapter we read as Paul was arrested in Israel and was shipped to Rome. During this time he was put on house arrest and continued to write.

> "To God's holy people in Ephesus, the faithful in Christ Jesus: Grace and peace to you from God our Father and the Lord Jesus Christ. Praise be to

> the God and Father of our Lord Jesus Christ, who has blessed us in the heavenly realms with every spiritual blessing in Christ. For he chose us in him before the creation of the world to be holy and blameless in his sight. In love he predestined us for adoption to sonship through Jesus Christ, in accordance with his pleasure and will—to the praise of his glorious grace, which he has freely given us in the One he loves." Ephesians 1:1-6 NIV

We have been called sons and daughters of the One who created everything. We've been adopted! Satan has tried so steadily to keep us from our inheritance, but God is stronger.

> "Because of his great love for us, God, who is rich in mercy, made us alive with Christ even when we were dead in transgressions—it is by grace you have been saved. And God raised us up with Christ and seated us with him in the heavenly realms in Christ Jesus, in order that in the coming ages he might show the incomparable riches of his grace, expressed in his kindness to us in Christ Jesus. For it is by grace you have been saved, through faith— and this is not from yourselves, it is the gift of God— not by works, so that no one can boast. For we are God's handiwork, created in Christ Jesus to do good works, which God prepared in advance for us to do." Ephesians 2:4-10 NIV

This calling is not to be taken lightly. We, who have given our lives over to Christ, have been saved by faith through grace. Paul called the church in Ephesus to speak and act with holiness. We have been set apart from the world. And if this is the case, we shouldn't look like the world. This goes for us as individuals and in how we lead our families. Christ ought to be the center of every family.

But all of this is easier said than done. Just like with anything, living a holy life requires tools.

> *"Stand firm then, with the belt of truth buckled around your waist, with the breastplate of righteousness in place, and with your feet fitted with the readiness that comes from the gospel of peace. In addition to all this, take up the shield of faith, with which you can extinguish all the flaming arrows of the evil one. Take the helmet of salvation and the sword of the Spirit, which is the word of God. And pray in the Spirit on all occasions with all kinds of prayers and requests. With this in mind, be alert and always keep on praying for all the Lord's people." Ephesians 6:14-18 NIV*

PHILIPPIANS. Philippi held a special place in Paul's heart. In writing the church there he starts off his letter with great joy and thanksgiving. The church had become aware of his imprisonment, but he shared with them that his chains had actually helped advance his ministry. He was sharing the good news with all the palace guards and everyone he came in contact with. And everyone knew he was in chains for Christ. Nothing was going to stop him from teaching . . . not even chains.

To follow Christ doesn't mean our lives will be cushy. Paul was in prison for God's sake! But in every situation we are to live a life worthy of the gospel of Christ.

> *"In your relationships with one another, have the same mindset as Christ Jesus: Who, being in very nature God, did not consider equality with God something to be used to his own advantage; rather, he made himself nothing by taking the very nature of a servant, being made in human likeness. And being found in appearance as a man, he humbled himself by becoming obedient to*

death—even death on a cross!" Philippians 2:5-8 NIV

"Rejoice in the Lord always. I will say it again: Rejoice! Let your gentleness be evident to all. The Lord is near. Do not be anxious about anything, but in every situation, by prayer and petition, with thanksgiving, present your requests to God. And the peace of God, which transcends all understanding, will guard your hearts and your minds in Christ Jesus.

Finally, brothers and sisters, whatever is true, whatever is noble, whatever is right, whatever is pure, whatever is lovely, whatever is admirable—if anything is excellent or praiseworthy—think about such things. Whatever you have learned or received or heard from me, or seen in me—put it into practice. And the God of peace will be with you." Philippians 4:4-9 NIV

PHILEMON. Paul was all about evangelism. He wanted to reach as many people with the gospel in his lifetime as possible. While reading Paul's letters we see him writing to churches and to his colleagues he'd placed in ministry. But the letter to Philemon is different. It looks a lot more like a letter of recommendation than anything else.

While imprisoned in Rome, Paul met a man named Onesimus. The two seemed to have become fairly close, but there was one problem: he was a runaway slave.

Slavery during that time period was an occupation. And much like today, when we work a job, we have duties to fulfill. In Onesimus' case, instead of fulfilling his duty . . . he took money from his boss and ran away. In finding this out, Paul knew what he had to do. He got out a piece of paper and began to write Philemon, Onesimus' master, whom he actually knew.

> "It is as none other than Paul—an old man and now also a prisoner of Christ Jesus—that I appeal to you for my son Onesimus, who became my son while I was in chains. Formerly he was useless to you, but now he has become useful both to you and to me.
>
> I am sending him—who is my very heart—back to you. I would have liked to keep him with me so that he could take your place in helping me while I am in chains for the gospel. But I did not want to do anything without your consent, so that any favor you do would not seem forced but would be voluntary. Perhaps the reason he was separated from you for a little while was that you might have him back forever—no longer as a slave, but better than a slave, as a dear brother. He is very dear to me but even dearer to you, both as a fellow man and as a brother in the Lord.
>
> So if you consider me a partner, welcome him as you would welcome me. If he has done you any wrong or owes you anything, charge it to me" Philemon 9-17 NIV

Can you imagine being Onesimus in this story? First of all, he stole from his boss and ran away. Then Paul wrote his boss a letter and Onesimus had to walk it back to him. *Will he take me back? Will he kill me?*

These were probably thoughts running through his head. But the most beautiful thing that comes out of this story is that before meeting Paul, Onesimus felt useless. Paul even addressed this in the letter. But now he is useful in the Kingdom of God. For that reason alone this letter has withstood the ages. Even if you feel like you have nothing to offer . . . God will use you to do great things.

COLOSSIANS. The church in Colossae was under attack by false teachers trying to distort their theology by overcomplicating the gospel. Though Paul didn't know the church in Colossae, his friend Epaphras knew the church very well and told him of their distress.

Paul's first order of business was to correct the church's theology of Christ.

> *"The Son is the image of the invisible God, the firstborn over all creation. For in him all things were created: things in heaven and on earth, visible and invisible, whether thrones or powers or rulers or authorities; all things have been created through him and for him. He is before all things, and in him all things hold together. And he is the head of the body, the church; he is the beginning and the firstborn from among the dead, so that in everything he might have the supremacy. For God was pleased to have all his fullness dwell in him, and through him to reconcile to himself all things, whether things on earth or things in heaven, by making peace through his blood, shed on the cross.*
>
> *So then, just as you received Christ Jesus as Lord, continue to live your lives in him, rooted and built up in him, strengthened in the faith as you were taught, and overflowing with thankfulness.*
>
> *See to it that no one takes you captive through hollow and deceptive philosophy, which depends on human tradition and the elemental spiritual forces of this world rather than on Christ." Colossians 1:15-20; 2:6-8 NIV*

This was Paul's major reason for writing his letter. The rest of the letter looks like Ephesians, focusing on living a Christian life and leading Christ-centered families.

This letter ends much like all the other letters do. Paul told his readers who would be delivering their letter. And in this case, Onesimus (the former slave) is one of the deliverers. Apparently, Philemon listened to Paul and found him useful.

1 TIMOTHY. A major portion of Paul's work was establishing leaders in the churches that he visited.

Paul knew Timothy since the beginning of his second missionary journey. They traveled all across Greece and Asia. Timothy saw firsthand how Paul did ministry. But the time had come for Timothy to take on a church all by himself and Ephesus was the place.

He was young. He was timid.
But Paul believed in him.

First order of business was to stop people from sharing false doctrines. Some people within the church wanted to be teachers of the law but didn't know what they were talking about.

Secondly, Paul addressed the leadership in the Ephesian church. Poor leadership was their biggest problem. The wrong people were in leadership and the church lacked proper care for its community.

First, the lead minister over the church.

> "Whoever aspires to be an overseer desires a noble task. Now the overseer is to be above re-

> *proach, faithful to his wife, temperate, self-controlled, respectable, hospitable, able to teach, not given to drunkenness, not violent but gentle, not quarrelsome, not a lover of money. He must manage his own family well and see that his children obey him, and he must do so in a manner worthy of full respect. (If anyone does not know how to manage his own family, how can he take care of God's church?) He must not be a recent convert, or he may become conceited and fall under the same judgment as the devil. He must also have a good reputation with outsiders, so that he will not fall into disgrace and into the devil's trap." 1 Timothy 3:1-7 NIV*

Next, the deacon.

> *"In the same way, deacons are to be worthy of respect, sincere, not indulging in much wine, and not pursuing dishonest gain. They must keep hold of the deep truths of the faith with a clear conscience. They must first be tested; and then if there is nothing against them, let them serve as deacons.*
>
> *A deacon must be faithful to his wife and must manage his children and his household well. Those who have served well gain an excellent standing and great assurance in their faith in Christ Jesus." 1 Timothy 3:8-10,12-13 NIV*

Paul finished his letter to Timothy with a final charge. *Flee from all that is sinful and pursue righteousness.*

> *"Fight the good fight of the faith. Take hold of the eternal life to which you were called when you made your good confession in the presence of many witnesses." 1 Timothy 6:12 NIV*

THE LETTERS

1 PETER. Peter's letter was to Christ followers scattered throughout Asia. The overarching message of this letter was to live Godly lives even in the midst of persecution.

But Peter reminds us that we are part of a royal family. We have hope when the world around us seems to be crashing down.

> "But you are a chosen people, a royal priesthood, a holy nation, God's special possession, that you may declare the praises of him who called you out of darkness into his wonderful light. Once you were not a people, but now you are the people of God; once you had not received mercy, but now you have received mercy.
>
> Dear friends, I urge you, as foreigners and exiles, to abstain from sinful desires, which wage war against your soul. Live such good lives among the pagans that, though they accuse you of doing wrong, they may see your good deeds and glorify God on the day he visits us." 1 Peter 2:9-12 NIV

TITUS. Titus was a friend and helper of Paul. He led a church on the Greek island of Crete and received a letter similar to the first letter Timothy received in Ephesus. Paul wanted to be sure the church had a solid foundation of leaders so he sent Titus a list of qualifications.

> "An elder must be blameless, faithful to his wife, a man whose children believe and are not open to the charge of being wild and disobedient. Since an overseer manages God's household, he must be blameless—not overbearing, not quick-tempered, not given to drunkenness, not violent, not pursuing dishonest gain. Rather, he must be hospitable, one who loves what is good, who is self-controlled, upright, holy and disciplined. He must hold firmly to

> *the trustworthy message as it has been taught, so that he can encourage others by sound doctrine and refute those who oppose it." Titus 1:6-9 NIV*

But this doesn't just go for the leaders of the church. Every member must live out their faith.

> *"For the grace of God has appeared that offers salvation to all people. It teaches us to say "No" to ungodliness and worldly passions, and to live self-controlled, upright and godly lives in this present age, while we wait for the blessed hope—the appearing of the glory of our great God and Savior, Jesus Christ, who gave himself for us to redeem us from all wickedness and to purify for himself a people that are his very own, eager to do what is good." Titus 2:11-14 NIV*

2 TIMOTHY. As Paul's life was coming to an end, he sent Timothy one final letter. Like a father writing his son one last time, Paul's letter can be summed up in this final charge.

> *"Preach the word; be prepared in season and out of season; correct, rebuke and encourage—with great patience and careful instruction. For the time will come when people will not put up with sound doctrine. Instead, to suit their own desires, they will gather around them a great number of teachers to say what their itching ears want to hear. They will turn their ears away from the truth and turn aside to myths. But you, keep your head in all situations, endure hardship, do the work of an evangelist, discharge all the duties of your ministry.*
>
> *For I am already being poured out like a drink offering, and the time for my departure is near. I have fought the good fight, I have finished the race, I*

> have kept the faith. Now there is in store for me the crown of righteousness, which the Lord, the righteous Judge, will award to me on that day—and not only to me, but also to all who have longed for his appearing." 2 Timothy 4:2-8 NIV

2 PETER. Peter's first letter addressed the persecution of the church in Asia. His second letter dealt with problems arising in the church itself. False teaching was becoming so rampant that the gospel itself was being blurred.

> "For this very reason, make every effort to add to your faith goodness; and to goodness, knowledge; and to knowledge, self-control; and to self-control, perseverance; and to perseverance, godliness; and to godliness, mutual affection; and to mutual affection, love. For if you possess these qualities in increasing measure, they will keep you from being ineffective and unproductive in your knowledge of our Lord Jesus Christ." 2 Peter 1:5-8 NIV

> "Above all, you must understand that in the last days scoffers will come, scoffing and following their own evil desires. They will say, "Where is this 'coming' he promised? Ever since our ancestors died, everything goes on as it has since the beginning of creation."

> But do not forget this one thing, dear friends: With the Lord a day is like a thousand years, and a thousand years are like a day. The Lord is not slow in keeping his promise, as some understand slowness. Instead he is patient with you, not wanting anyone to perish, but everyone to come to repentance." 2 Peter 3:3-4, 8-9 NIV

HEBREWS. Though we don't know who wrote Hebrews for sure, we do know that it was written to calm the fears of persecuted Christians who were reverting back to Judaism for fear of their lives.

The author of Hebrews walked his Israelite readers through the Old Testament proclaiming Jesus as the Son of God. It sounds a little like this: *Jesus is superior to the Angels, High Priests and Prophets! He is our greatest High Priest and His blood eternally cleanses us from our sins.*

> *"Therefore, brothers and sisters, since we have confidence to enter the Most Holy Place by the blood of Jesus, by a new and living way opened for us through the curtain, that is, his body, and since we have a great priest over the house of God, let us draw near to God with a sincere heart and with the full assurance that faith brings, having our hearts sprinkled to cleanse us from a guilty conscience and having our bodies washed with pure water. Let us hold unswervingly to the hope we profess, for he who promised is faithful. And let us consider how we may spur one another on toward love and good deeds, not giving up meeting together, as some are in the habit of doing, but encouraging one another" Hebrews 10:19-25 NIV*

JUDE. It's so sad how often we see false teachers creeping in and distorting Jesus' gospel. Jude wrote his letter to believers to help them stay strong in their faith and not be swayed.

> *"Dear friends, although I was very eager to write to you about the salvation we share, I felt compelled to write and urge you to contend for the faith that was once for all entrusted to God's holy people. For certain individuals whose condemnation was written about long ago have secretly slipped in among you. They are ungodly people, who pervert the grace of our God into a license for immo-*

> rality and deny Jesus Christ our only Sovereign and Lord.
>
> But you, dear friends, by building yourselves up in your most holy faith and praying in the Holy Spirit, keep yourselves in God's love as you wait for the mercy of our Lord Jesus Christ to bring you to eternal life. Be merciful to those who doubt; save others by snatching them from the fire; to others show mercy, mixed with fear—hating even the clothing stained by corrupted flesh." Jude 3-4, 20-23 NIV

1 JOHN. The apostle John spent many years in Ephesus where he made strong relationships with the surrounding churches in Asia Minor. He wrote his letter to strengthen the churches with spiritual truths and to discredit false teachings.

> "God is light; in him there is no darkness at all. If we claim to have fellowship with him and yet walk in the darkness, we lie and do not live out the truth. But if we walk in the light, as he is in the light, we have fellowship with one another, and the blood of Jesus, his Son, purifies us from all sin.
>
> My dear children, I write this to you so that you will not sin. But if anybody does sin, we have an advocate with the Father—Jesus Christ, the Righteous One. He is the atoning sacrifice for our sins, and not only for ours but also for the sins of the whole world." 1 John 1:5-7; 2:1-2 NIV

John wanted his readers to understand that every choice boils down to two options: Good or Evil.

> "I write these things to you who believe in the name of the Son of God so that you may know that you have eternal life." 1 John 5:13 NIV

2 JOHN. His second letter is short, sweet and to the point. John urged his readers to be careful around false teachers. If their message didn't line up with his, they shouldn't be shown hospitality.

> "If anyone comes to you and does not bring this teaching, do not take them into your house or welcome them. Anyone who welcomes them shares in their wicked work." 2 John 10-11 NIV

3 JOHN. In John's third letter he addresses two things. First, he commended his friend Gaius' for his hospitality. Second, he called out a man names Diotrephes for being prideful and not accepting other people's Christ-centered teachings. In his frustration, he called the church to pursue hospitality and not imitate Diotrephes.

> "Dear friend, do not imitate what is evil but what is good. Anyone who does what is good is from God. Anyone who does what is evil has not seen God." 3 John 11 NIV

REVELATION

CHAPTER SIXTEEN

Blessed is the one who reads aloud the words of this prophecy, and blessed are those who hear it and take to heart what is written in it, because the time is near.
Revelation 1:3 NIV

This final book has caused many people over the years to steer clear of ever reading it. It's full of imagery and categorized as Apocalyptic. But don't let that scare you off because it's full of redemption and completes the story.

Before we dive into this book, let's talk a little bit about how to read it. We're about to embark on a journey through dense imagery of the Spiritual realm. Much of it is difficult to comprehend, but at the heart of it all is this: from the Creation of time God has loved His people yet they have continuously rejected Him. Their rejection comes at a cost, which Christ paid Himself as a gift. But some reject that gift.

JOHN THE REVELATOR

WRITE. It was around year 95 AD. Approximately sixty years after Jesus had ascended into Heaven and He appeared before John the apostle.

> *"Write on a scroll what you see and send it to the seven churches: to Ephesus, Smyrna, Pergamum, Thyatira, Sardis, Philadelphia and Laodicea." Revelation 1:11 NIV*

John could do nothing else but fall at His feet. He felt dead.

> *"Do not be afraid. I am the First and the Last. I am the Living One; I was dead, and now look, I am alive forever and ever! And I hold the keys of death and Hades. Write, therefore, what you have seen, what is now and what will take place later." Revelation 1:17-19 NIV*

Jesus gave John specific letters to write to seven churches in Asia Minor to build them up.

To Ephesus, you hate wickedness but you lack love!
To Smyrna, be faithful through persecution!
To Pergamum, repent and follow me!
To Thyatira, repent and follow me!
To Sardis, your faith is dead. Wake up and follow me!
To Philadelphia, keep holding on to me!
To Laodicea, you're lukewarm; neither good nor evil.

JUDGMENT AND CONSEQUENCE

After this John looked and saw Heaven sitting before him. The throne room of God was before his very eyes.

He saw the seven churches represented by seven lamp stands. Seven angels represented by seven stars. There were twenty-four elders who were both kings and priests and around the throne were four living creatures covered with eyes. They never stopped praising God day and night.

Then John saw God sitting on His throne with a scroll in His hand sealed with seven seals. John looked high and low in Heaven and on earth but no one could open the scroll. In His distress, one of the elders pointed him to the Lion of Judah. But John saw a Lamb. The Lamb that was slain who is Jesus! Of course, He is the One! And when He grabbed it, the four creatures and twenty-four elders fell in worship.

> *"You are worthy to take the scroll and to open its seals, because you were slain, and with your blood you purchased for God persons from every tribe and language and people and nation. You have made them to be a kingdom and priests to serve our God, and they will reign on the earth." Revelation 5:9-10 NIV*

SEALS (6:1-17;8:1-5). Before John's very eyes, all of Heaven and Earth worshiped Jesus as He opened the scroll, seal by seal. The seals begin with humanity's disobedience and lead into their consequence.

Seal One unleashed a white horse out for battle.
Seal Two unleashed a red horse encouraging violence.
Seal Three unleashed a black horse symbolizing famine.
Seal Four unleashed a pale horse bringing death.
Seal Five displayed the souls of the persecuted.
Seal Six displayed an earthquake of God's wrath.
Seal Seven called for silence followed by judgment.

TRUMPETS (8:6-13; 11:15-19). As the seventh seal was opened, there was thirty minutes of silence in Heaven. Next, seven angels were given seven trumpets. Destruction fell on the earth as they sounded their instruments.

Trumpet One destroyed a third of the land.
Trumpet Two destroyed a third of the sea.
Trumpet Three destroyed a third of the water supply.
Trumpet Four dimmed a third of the earth's light.
Trumpet Five unleashed torment on unbelievers.
Trumpet Six unleashed an angelic army who killed a third of humanity. Still, the rest of humanity did not repent.
Trumpet Seven unleashed God's final judgment.

Gradually the torment became more and more severe. The earth was a warzone. Who would win? Good or evil? God sent two prophets to the earth but humanity rejected them and put them to death. But three and a half days later God brought them back to life and there was a severe earthquake killing seven thousand people.

This apparently got everyone's attention because the survivors gave God glory and began to worship Him.

> *The seventh angel sounded his trumpet, and there were loud voices in heaven, which said: The kingdom of the world has become the kingdom of our Lord and of his Messiah, and he will reign forever and ever.*
>
> *And the twenty-four elders, who were seated on their thrones before God, fell on their faces and worshiped God, saying: "We give thanks to you, Lord God Almighty, the One who is and who was, because you have taken your great power and have begun to reign. The nations were angry, and your wrath has come. The time has come for judging the dead, and for rewarding your servants the*

> *prophets and your people who revere your name, both great and small—and for destroying those who destroy the earth."*
>
> *Then God's temple in heaven was opened, and within his temple was seen the ark of his covenant. And there came flashes of lightning, rumblings, peals of thunder, an earthquake and a severe hailstorm. Revelation 11:15-19 NIV*

THE WOMAN AND THE BEAST. John then saw a woman crying out in pain about to give birth. This child was to rule all the nations. At first glance you might assume the mother is Mary. But, the imagery that Jesus is showing us is the relationship between Him and Israel.

Satan wanted the child dead. He fought to kill Him, but Heaven grabbed hold of the child and war broke out between Heaven and Hell. But Satan was too weak and fell to the earth.

> *"Rejoice, you heavens and you who dwell in them! But woe to the earth and the sea, because the devil has gone down to you! He is filled with fury, because he knows that his time is short." Revelation 12:12 NIV*

Satan couldn't destroy Heaven so he sought to destroy earth. He was crafty and deceiving. He performed great signs and was impressive. Now the people had to make a choice: God or Satan. It was one or the other.

THE THREE ANGELS. Then John saw three angels cry out in a loud voice. *Let every nation, tribe, language and people worship the One who created everything. Fear Him because His judgment is near. He has overcome the evil* one. *Anyone who worships darkness will answer to God's fury.*

SEVEN BOWLS (16:1-21). Despite God's judgment, some people continued to follow Satan. But their choice didn't go without consequence. Then John saw seven angels holding seven bowls of God's wrath ready to be poured out.

Bowl One unleashed terrible sores on the people.
Bowl Two turned the sea into blood killing all sea creatures.
Bowl Three turned rivers and springs to blood taking away their water supply.
Bowl Four scorched the people by intensifying the sun.
Bowl Five plunged Satan's kingdom into darkness and intensified the sores of the first bowl.
Bowl Six dried up the Euphrates River in preparation for the Battle of Armageddon.
Bowl Seven was poured out into the air. Lightning rumbled. A severe earthquake shook the earth. Large hailstones fell from the sky. God's wrath poured out on all who cursed Him. Then a loud voice from the throne of the temple exclaimed, *It is done!*

THE FINAL BATTLE. Throughout the entire story of the Bible we find good and evil at war. God continually gave humanity grace and a chance to return to Him. But Satan didn't want to loosen his grip.

> *"I saw heaven standing open and there before me was a white horse, whose rider is called Faithful and True. With justice he judges and wages war. His eyes are like blazing fire, and on his head are many crowns. He has a name written on him that no one knows but he himself. He is dressed in a robe dipped in blood, and his name is the Word of God. The armies of heaven were following him, rid-*

ing on white horses and dressed in fine linen, white and clean. Coming out of his mouth is a sharp sword with which to strike down the nations. He will rule them with an iron scepter. He treads the winepress of the fury of the wrath of God Almighty. On his robe and on his thigh he has this name written: King of Kings and Lord of Lords.

Then I saw the beast and the kings of the earth and their armies gathered together to wage war against the rider on the horse and his army. But the beast was captured, and with it the false prophet who had performed the signs on its behalf. With these signs he had deluded those who had received the mark of the beast and worshiped its image. The two of them were thrown alive into the fiery lake of burning sulfur. The rest were killed with the sword coming out of the mouth of the rider on the horse, and all the birds gorged themselves on their flesh." Revelation 19:11-16, 19-21 NIV

After this Satan would be thrown into the Abyss for one thousand years freeing the world from his deceit. After the thousand years he would be released from his prison and go out to deceive the world, but God would throw him back into Hell to be tormented day and night forever.

(Side Note: There are two major views of understanding the 1,000-year reign of Jesus: Premillennialism believes in a literal 1,000-year reign while Amillennialism does not.)

NEW HEAVEN AND NEW EARTH. Just as Satan will be judged, all of humanity will also be judged. Those who believe in God and worship Him will be rewarded. But those who reject Him will be punished and go their separate way for eternity.

> "I saw the Holy City, the new Jerusalem, coming down out of heaven from God, prepared as a bride beautifully dressed for her husband.
>
> Look! God's dwelling place is now among the people, and he will dwell with them. They will be his people, and God himself will be with them and be their God. He will wipe every tear from their eyes. There will be no more death or mourning or crying or pain, for the old order of things has passed away. He who was seated on the throne said, 'I am making everything new!'" Revelation 21:2-5 NIV

The New Heaven and New Earth will reflect God's original design: Goodness. It will be free from sin and Satan's rule.

As John looked around, he saw walls made of jasper and streets were paved with gold. There was no longer a use for a temple because God Almighty and Jesus is the temple. The tree of life was restored in Heaven, which sat in the original Garden of Eden. After thousands of years, God's creation was back as it was meant to be.

PRESENT DAY: 95 AD

After seeing all of these visions, reality set in and John began to write as Jesus spoke to him one last time.

> "Look, I am coming soon! My reward is with me, and I will give to each person according to what they have done. I am the Alpha and the Omega, the First and the Last, the Beginning and the End. I, Jesus, have sent my angel to give you this testimony for the churches. I am the Root and the

REVELATION

Offspring of David, and the bright Morning Star."
Revelation 22:12, 16 NIV

WHAT NEXT?

AFTERWORD

What now? You've finished studying the Bible all the way through (congrats, by the way! Not everyone can say that!).

But now what?

I want to encourage you to open up your Bible or go out and buy one if you don't have one. I love technology and phones have tons of Bible apps you can download now, but there's just something about holding the real thing. But either way, start reading the Bible. There are tons of Bible reading plans out there.

If you don't have a relationship with God, I want to encourage you to start talking to Him. Your first prayer might seem awkward, but He's already on the other side of the line. If it's been a while for you, right now is a good time to start.

Literally right now, don't read anymore. Go pray.
I told you to stop reading!

WHAT NEXT?

I have to settle with you. When I started the journey to write this book, I felt very unqualified. It was my first book. My life isn't all put together. My wife and I argue (but she always wins, she says). I get frustrated with people. I don't have the best prayer life. I'm not the most eloquent speaker or writer. But, as I read through the Bible from start to finish, I began to see myself within the story. God uses broken, frustrating, rich, poor, irritable, controversial, ineloquent, dirty people to do great things throughout the entire Bible. Maybe He can use me too.

No matter where you are in your life's journey, you're invited. You are loved. You are important. You have a story. You have a part to play in God's even greater story.

ABOUT THE AUTHOR

Chris Webber is a youth and worship minister holding degrees in Christian Education from Harding University and Dallas Theological Seminary. He is passionate about sharing God's love with the world alongside his lovely wife, Katie Sue. He currently lives in the Houston, TX area with his wife and son, Carson.

Urgent Plea:

Thank you so much for reading my book!

I really appreciate you for believing in this book and I'd love to hear what you thought about it! I need your input to help make sure the next version of this book is spectacular.

Please leave me a helpful review on Amazon letting me know your thoughts on the book.

Thank you so much!!

-Chris Webber

Made in the USA
San Bernardino, CA
14 June 2019